Capitalism

Short Histories of Big Ideas Series List

Capitalism

PAUL BOWLES

Harlow, England • London • New York • Boston • San Francisco • Toronto
Sydney • Tokyo • Singapore • Hong Kong • Seoul • Taipei • New Delhi
Cape Town • Madrid • Mexico City • Amsterdam • Munich • Paris • Milan

Pearson Education Limited

Edinburgh Gate
Harlow CM20 2JE
United Kingdom
Tel: +44 (0)1279 623623
Fax: +44 (0)1279 431059
Website: www.pearsoned.co.uk

First edition published in Great Britain in 2007

© Pearson Education Limited 2007

The right of Paul Bowles to be identified as author of this work
has been asserted by him in accordance with the Copyright, Designs
and Patents Act 1988.

ISBN 978-0-582-50609-1

British Library Cataloguing in Publication Data
A CIP catalogue record for this book can be obtained from the British Library

Library of Congress Cataloging in Publication Data
Bowles, Paul.
    Capitalism / Paul Bowles.
       p. cm.
    Includes bibliographical references and index.
    ISBN-13: 978-0-582-50609-1
    ISBN-10: 0-582-50609-3
    1. Capitalism. 2. Capitalism—History. I. Title.

HB501.B7378 2006
330.12'2—dc22

                             2006043567

10 9 8 7 6 5 4 3 2
10 09 08 07

Designed by Sue Lamble
Set by 35 in 9/15pt Iowan
Printed and bound in Malaysia (CTP -VVP)

The Publishers' policy is to use paper manufactured from sustainable forests.

To my parents

Contents

Series Editor's Preface

WHAT MAKES THE WORLD MOVE? Great men? Irresistible forces? Catastrophic events?

When listening to the morning news on the radio, reading our daily newspapers, following debates on the internet, watching evening television, all of these possibilities – and more – are offered as explanations of the troubles that beset the world in the Middle East, the "war on terror" in Iraq and Afghanistan, environmental disasters at Chernobyl or New Orleans, and genocide in Sudan or Rwanda.

Where should we look to find answers to the puzzles of the present? To psychology? To economics? To sociology? To political science? To philosophy? Each of these disciplines offer insights into the personalities and the subterranean forces that propel the events that change the world, and within each of these disciplines there are experts who dissect current affairs on the foundation of these insights.

But all of these events, these problems, and even these disciplines themselves have one thing in common: they have a history. And it is through an understanding of the history of those ideas that inspired the people behind the events, and the ideas behind the ideologies that attempted to explain and control the forces around them that we can comprehend the perplexing and confusing world of the present day.

"*Short Histories of Big Ideas*" aims to provide readers with clear, concise and readable explanations of those ideas that were instrumental in shaping the twentieth century and that continue to shape – and reshape – the present. Everyone who attempts to follow the events of today via newspapers, television, radio and the internet cannot help but see or hear references to "capitalism", "communism", "feminism", "environmentalism", "nationalism", "colonialism" and many other "isms". And, while most of us probably believe that we have a basic understanding of what these terms mean, we are probably much less certain about who it was that coined, invented or defined them. Even more murky is our understanding of how these concepts moved from an idea to become an ideology and, perhaps, a phenomenon that changed the world. Most bewildering may be the disputes and controversies between factions and divisions within the movements and political parties that claim to be the true followers and the legitimate heirs of those who first conceived of the concepts to which they claim to adhere.

The authors of these *Short Histories* have been asked to write accessible, jargon-free prose with the goal of making comprehensible to the intelligent, interested but non-expert reader these highly complicated concepts. In each instance the approach taken is chronological, as each author attempts to explain the origins of these ideas, to describe the people who created them and then to follow the twisting path they followed from conception to the present. Each author in the series is an expert in the field, with a mastery of the literature on the subject – and a desire to convey to readers the knowledge and the understanding that the research of specialist scholars has produced, but which is normally inaccessible to those not engaged in studying these subjects in an academic environment.

The work of specialists often seems remote, obscure, even pedantic, to the non-specialist, but the authors in this series are committed to the goal of bringing the insights and understanding of specialists to a wider public, to concerned citizens and general readers who wish to go beyond today's headlines and form a more comprehensive and meaningful picture of today's world.

Gordon Martel
Series Editor

Acknowledgements

THIS BOOK HAS BEEN MANY YEARS in the making. In fact, well before I knew I was going to write it. For most of the past 30 years, starting as a young undergraduate, I have been reading and thinking about capitalism. There are therefore many teachers, colleagues and friends who have shaped my thoughts and to whom I owe my thanks. Here I can only mention a few colleagues with whom I have shared many conversations over recent years: Osvaldo Croci, Xiaoyuan Dong, Elie Korkmaz, Brian MacLean, Tony Stone, the late Gordon White, and Henry Veltmeyer.

The book was largely written while on sabbatical at the University of Adelaide. I am grateful to the University for providing such a pleasant environment within which to write. A small group of colleagues there – Ray Broomhill, Steven Barrett, Ken Bridge and Pat Wright – joined me for a discussion of the first draft of the book and provided many valuable comments. Other colleagues, Mark Beeson and Barbara Harriss-White, also read the whole manuscript and were generous with their insights. All of these discussions reinforced for me the fact that how a book on "capitalism" is written is an intensely personal choice. They made me work through more fully exactly what it was that I wanted to say in *"Capitalism"*. In this, I was also encouraged by the series editor, Gordon Martel, who read the first draft and wanted to see more of "me" in the final version. To all of these people, I offer my thanks for their comments and for enabling and encouraging me to set out my own views more clearly.

My partner, Fiona MacPhail, provided not only insightful comments on the book but also supported my efforts whenever needed. I am grateful for her advice, her encouragement and for always being there.

This book is dedicated to my parents, Geoff and Irene. They have lived through a good part of the twists and turns of capitalism that are discussed in this book. I hope that this book's theorizing of capitalism resonates with some of their experiences.

Timeline

1492   Columbus "discovers" the Americas. European
expansion creates a world "capitalist" market.

1600s   The European peasantry is gradually removed from
the land.

1750s   The Industrial Revolution begins in England and
then spreads to Western Europe and, later, to North
America. A "working class" is formed in the
industrializing capitalist countries.

1848   Revolutions sweep Europe as the working classes
and the rising capitalist classes make demands for
new forms of political organization.

1870s   European colonial expansion spreads to include much
of Africa and Asia. Colonialism spurs this wave of
"globalization".

1914   European powers go to war. The First World War.

1917   The first of the twentieth century's "state socialist
revolutions" occurs in Russia. The scope of capitalism
is, for the first time, geographically shrunken.

1929   The Wall Street Crash.

1930s   The Great Depression haunts Western Europe and
North America and its effects are felt throughout the
rest of the capitalist world.

1945   The Second World War ends with a new international economic order established which produces capitalism's "Golden Age".

1973   The "Golden Age" fizzles out as high oil prices and US unilateral economic policy bring post-war Keynesianism to an end.

1980s   A shift to the political right in Britain and the US ushers in a new period of neoliberal policies which strengthens capital. Developing countries are caught in the debt crisis and implement neoliberal policies as part of the World Bank's Structural Adjustment Programs.

1989   The Berlin Wall falls signalling the collapse of the Soviet system. Capitalism regains its global reach and a new phase of "globalization" begins.

1990s   Financial crises return with global capitalism affecting countries in Europe in 1992, Mexico in 1994, Asia in 1997, Brazil and Russia in 1998, and Argentina in 2001.

1999   The "Battle of Seattle" marks the moment when the "anti-capitalism" movement gets the attention of world leaders and policy-makers. It signifies the battle of ideas over the future of "global capitalism", a battle which continues to be played out as evident by the protests in cities across the world wherever world leaders meet.

Who's Who

John Locke

Writing in the mid-1600s Locke presents the argument that the fruits of one's own labour can justly be claimed as private property.

Adam Smith

His famous book, *The Wealth of Nations*, was published in 1776 and established Smith as a classic advocate of the free market system. His name has been invoked ever since to proclaim the superiority of the capitalist system.

Karl Marx and Friedrich Engels

As industrial capitalism expanded so did its critics. The two most famous were Marx and Engels who argued that capitalism needed to be overthrown and that humans would only be free when a classless society was established. State socialist revolutions throughout the twentieth century claimed adherence to their work.

Lenin

Leader of the October Revolution in Russia in 1917, Lenin argued that the highest stage of capitalism was Imperialism. When this stage was reached (global) capitalism would lead to inter-imperialist wars.

John Maynard Keynes

British economist whose ideas were credited with bringing about capitalism's "Golden Age". He advocated government intervention to stabilize the economy and to avoid a repeat of the disaster of the Great Depression. The influence of his work waned in the 1970s as Keynesian policies appeared to have no answer to the problems of inflation and unemployment which began to afflict the advanced capitalist economies.

J.K. Galbraith

US economist famous for his analysis of modern capitalism as being run by a "technocracy" associated with large corporations. Advocated a significant role for government in controlling corporate interests and in distributing income.

Milton Friedman

Along with Friedrich von Hayek, he was the intellectual force behind the shift to neoliberal policies in Britain and the US in the 1980s. A believer in restricted roles for government and for greater use of private markets.

Francis Fukuyama

Rose to international fame when he predicted that the collapse of communism in 1989 represented "the end of history". Capitalism had won and would remain dominant forever.

James Tobin

US economist whose name is associated with the "Tobin tax", a rallying cry for the opponents of global capitalism who would like to see the power of international financial speculators reduced by taxing the short-term purchase of foreign exchange.

CHAPTER 1

How to think about capitalism

Introduction

CAPITALISM HAS PROVED ITSELF TO be the most enduring economic system of our time. After a century of failed challenges to its dominance – from state socialist economies such as the former Soviet Union – the vast majority of the world's population now lives in capitalist economies. However, despite its contemporary dominance, capitalism remains contested. World organizations such as the World Bank and the International Monetary Fund (IMF) and many world leaders promise that global capitalism will bring prosperity to us all. Meanwhile, "anti-globalization" movements have been evident on the streets of major world cities from Seattle to Hong Kong, arguing that global capitalism will only bring more poverty and more environmental degradation and give more power to corporations. Capitalism is pervasive and regulates the daily lives of billions. Capitalism generates passion and sparks opposition. But how does capitalism work?

Capitalism certainly has daily familiarity. We are continually exhorted, by the close to half a trillion US dollars spent worldwide annually on advertising,[1] to buy this good or that good. Television channels find it necessary to inform us at hourly intervals of the latest gyrations of the stock market. The influence of capitalism can be found everywhere, including in our language – we "spend" time, we "value" friendships, we "earn" respect. Even the mundane world of national income accounting is influenced, for example in what we count as "economic activity" – anything performed in the market sphere – and excludes other activities, such as working in the home. And yet, despite this pervasiveness, capitalism's workings remain obscure. Why do we find works which offer us expositions on the "logic" or the "essence" of capitalism or the solution to its "mystery"?[2] Why should capitalism require expositions of this kind? Why isn't it obvious what capitalism is and how it works?

One reason is simply that capitalism appears in a variety of guises across countries. For example, it has been described as "gangster capitalism" in present-day Russia, as "welfare capitalism" in Nordic countries, as *"laissez-faire* capitalism" in Hong Kong, as "crony capitalism" in parts of Asia and Latin America, and as "petro-diamond capitalism" in Angola; and yet all are still capitalism. Capitalism not only varies across space, it also changes through time. For example, seventeenth century "merchant capital" is in many ways vastly different from the "digital capitalism" of the twenty-first century; and yet, there are constants too.[3]

Part of the challenge of understanding capitalism is therefore precisely that it is capable of exhibiting great variation across countries and through time and yet still retaining the common elements that enable all its varieties, spatial and temporal, to be similar at root. Capitalism, as a form of economic organization, is simultaneously adaptable, flexible and evolving but also contains constant and unchanging central features.

Another reason for the opaqueness of capitalism despite its daily familiarity is that, while capitalism has been described in the variety of ways just illustrated, it has also been a term that has been avoided. "Capitalism" is, as one commentator has noted, "a funny word". As he explains, "just using the word – otherwise a neutral enough designation for an economic and social system on whose properties all sides agree – seemed to position you in a vaguely critical, suspicious, if not outright socialist stance: only committed right-wing ideologues and full-throated market apologists also use it with the same relish" (Jameson 1991: xxi). Many have not wished be so positioned – as either "suspicious socialists" or "market apologists". Capitalism has therefore been subject to "non-naming". It is common to find a variety of terms to describe the contemporary world: the "information age", "post-industrial society", the "free market economy", the "global economy", the "postmodern or post-colonial world", the "consumer society" or the "network society", to name but some of them. In all of these terms, the word "capitalism" is conspicuous by its absence; and yet, all of them implicitly presuppose a capitalist economy.

To these reasons we must add a further explanation: capitalism is well practised in the art of concealing its workings. That is, we are invited to see the goods that the capitalist economy produces simply as objects and not as the products of labour and resources. Our lives as consumers and as producers are somehow divided. Accepting this division has been described by Marxists as "commodity fetishism", as viewing goods as providing us with some particular qualities – glamour, sex appeal or whatever – rather than as seeing them as the output of a process of production involving people. Indeed, social activist and big business critic Naomi Klein (2000) has argued that we are increasingly being urged to define ourselves by our allegiance to particular corporate brand names – as a Nike or as an Adidas person, or as a Mac or an IBM devotee, for example.

If we did think of goods as the outputs of processes involving people, we might be inclined to ask who these people are, under what conditions do they work, and what are the environmental consequences of producing these goods. In general, capitalist societies do not encourage us to ask these types of questions. True, there are some exceptions: the "Fair Trade" movement, supported by organizations such as Oxfam, has tried to impress upon us that as consumers we should be aware of working conditions and wage levels. We can then use our power as consumers to purchase those brands which pay their workers a "fair wage", whether it be picking coffee or making souvenirs. The "no sweatshop" campaigns in the clothing industry provide another example of the attempts to make us view goods as the outcomes of social processes. But such campaigns face an uphill task. Capitalism simply finds it necessary – and easier – to bombard us with glossy images of satisfied consumers rather than to encourage us to dwell on production conditions and consequences.[4] Winner of an "Alternative Nobel Prize" in 1993, Indian activist Vandana Shiva (2000: 112, italics added) has gone as far as to argue that "we enter the next millennium with a *deliberate production of ignorance* about ecological risks such as the deregulation of environmental protection and the destruction of ecologically sustainable life-styles for peasant, tribal, pastoral and craft communities across the Third World".

Given these reasons why capitalism can be regarded as opaque despite its daily familiarity, it is now possible to deduce how to think about capitalism and what questions should be answered. When thinking about capitalism, three central issues need to be addressed. Firstly, what is capitalism and how does it function in an abstract way? That is, to identify the constants, the defining characteristics, of capitalism, and what they imply about the way capitalism operates. Secondly, why is it that capitalism generates such passion both for and against, to the extent that mere mention of the term is often avoided? That is, to examine the case for capitalism as a form of social and economic organization and to analyse why others view it as a form of organization which must be replaced. Thirdly, what are the variations of capitalism over time and space?

Thinking about capitalism requires us to think at several levels, as Box 1.1 indicates. We must think *abstractly* to identify capitalism's central features, and think *historically* to chart variations over time and space. We also need to think *normatively* about how the present capitalist system works, that is, how desirable it

---

BOX 1.1

How to think about capitalism

1 *Abstractly* – to identify defining characteristics.

2 *Normatively* – to assess strengths and weaknesses.

3 *Historically* – to see the variations over time and space.

---

is as a system for the organization of life, in order to understand the passion that it generates both for and against.

Outline of the book

These three levels determine the structure of this book. In the remainder of this chapter, I will set out the central features of capitalism, that is, identify and analyse *abstractly* those constant characteristics which are the defining features of capitalism. I will also discuss some of the ways of thinking about the periodization of capitalism, that is, the ways in which capitalism's evolution over time have been interpreted.

In Chapters 2 and 3, I will present the *normative* arguments and review the cases for and against capitalism. I will present these cases through the ideas of some of the major analysts of capitalism, starting with works from the past such as those of Adam Smith and Karl Marx. There is a problem in starting from here, since the "capitalism" which Smith analysed in the late eighteenth century and that analysed by Marx in the mid-nineteenth century differ in very significant ways from that which we observe at the beginning of the twenty-first century. However, it is not possible to launch into an analysis of contemporary capitalism without first knowing something of its evolution and, equally importantly, knowing something about the early writers whose analyses have profoundly influenced the ways in which subsequent thinkers have approached the topic of capitalism. Chapter 2 presents the arguments made by the supporters of capitalism who view it as a system which is "natural" and which makes us "free". This is followed, in Chapter 3, with an overview of the arguments of those who view capitalism as a system which is better described as "unjust" and "unstable", and a discussion of the arguments which they have advanced for either the reform or the replacement of capitalism.

Chapters 1, 2 and 3 are mainly concerned with the analysis of capitalism as an abstract system. The rest of the book analyses capitalism *historically*. Chapters 4, 5 and 6 consider how capitalism has worked in particular societies. Here I will examine the forms that capitalism has taken in different countries (such as Japan and the United States). I will examine how capitalism has performed over the twentieth century with its periods of growth and recession. These three chapters therefore analyse variations of capitalism over time and space.

In Chapter 7, I will examine what we should make of the contemporary phase of capitalism, that of "global capitalism". Is this a new stage of capitalism in which states are increasingly weakened in the face powerful international market forces? Or is this a huge exaggeration and nation states are still powerful? Should we think of global capitalism as a new form of imperialism? Or is regionalism really a more accurate description of the contemporary world?

Throughout the book, capitalism is analysed as a *system*. The "capitalist system" is introduced as an abstract process, meaning that is has requirements and dynamics. The capitalist system is also introduced as a historical process, evolving over time in response to various pressures and forces. This idea of capitalism as a "system" implies that its various parts are tied together by a set of processes which can be understood in a reasonably coherent way; it is precisely for this reason that many have sought to identify its "logic" or "inner workings". Search for underlying "truths" or "logics" is, according to some, a false search. It is likely to conceal more than it reveals and to impose commonalities where really there are only differences. This view, popular in contemporary social science under the banner of "post-structuralism", is not one that is accepted here. Instead, I will argue that capitalism can and should be analysed as a "system".

One implication of viewing capitalism as a "system" is that it consists of interrelated parts. This enables us to see that the acts of consumption and production are part of the same process rather than separate activities; that is, it enables us to transcend "commodity fetishism". It also means that the "capitalist system" must be viewed as not only an economic system; although economic processes must be a central focus of any analysis of capitalism, other political and social processes also constitute parts of the "system". This will become evident in the following chapters as the relationships between capitalism and democracy and between capitalism and social equity, to give two examples, are examined.

The capitalist system: a simple definition and some not-so-simple issues arising from it

What is capitalism? or, more precisely, "what is the capitalist system"? As noted above, Jameson (1991: xxi) argues that capitalism is "an economic and social system on whose properties all sides agree". There is considerable truth in this, but the answer to my question is more complex than Jameson suggests. To start with the easy part, capitalism is a system for organizing production which is based upon the institutions of private property and the market, and which relies upon the pursuit of private profit as its driving force.

BOX 1.2

Capitalism: the defining characteristics

A form of economic organization based on:

1 *Private ownership* of firms and society's productive assets.

2 The *market*, that is, the voluntary purchase and sale of goods, services and factors of production such as land, labour and capital.

3 The *profit motive* as the driving force.

This is a relatively simple and straightforward definition which would not cause controversy. At this level, Jameson is right and this definition would secure widespread agreement; Box 1.2 is not controversial. However, if we delve a little deeper, then some points of contention do arise, contentions which have less to do with the definition of capitalism as a system in the abstract and more to do with its historical evolution. Let us briefly review some of these contentious points, starting with private ownership.

"Ownership" is, in fact, a complex concept. It may seem obvious what is meant by the statement "the factory is privately owned", but it is perhaps only obvious because we are used to hearing the term. If we ask "who owns the modern factory?" the answer is not so obvious. Is it owned by the factory manager? The Board of Directors to whom he or she reports? The millions of individual shareholders who might own shares in the company but who never attend the company's Annual General Meeting? The pension fund managers who buy shares on behalf of individuals they have never seen?

"Ownership" is best thought of as a "bundle" of property rights such as the right to use assets, the right to sell or transfer them, and the right to the income stream generated by those assets. Seen in this light, the modern corporation is owned by the shareholders in the sense that they claim the income from the use of company assets. However, they delegate the right to use the assets on a day-to-day basis to CEOs – a right which can be withdrawn if the shareholders are not satisfied with the performance of the managers in managing their assets. In the small firm, it is often the manager who is the owner and all ownership rights are vested in one individual. But whatever the size of the company, it is private individuals who own the productive assets of the private firm.

An economy in which most firms are privately owned is typically said to be a capitalist economy. The qualifying word "typically" is added here because even in cases where the private ownership of productive assets dominates, some writers are still reluctant to classify economies as "capitalist" if other conditions are not met. An example of this is the case of fascist societies. Are they capitalist? The extensive private ownership of capital would indicate that they are. Nobel Prize-winning economist Milton Friedman supports this view. He regards, for example, 1930s fascist Italy and Spain as "fundamentally capitalist" since "private enterprise was the dominant form of economic organization" (1962: 10). However, not everyone agrees. Because of fascism's subjugation of the individual to the collective, the dominance of private property is not regarded as sufficient to conclude that the country is capitalist. Thus, eminent MIT economist Lester Thurow (1996: 5), for example, writes that "on December 8, 1941, when the United States entered World

War II, the United States and Britain were essentially the only capitalistic countries left on the face of the earth and Britain was on the edge of military defeat. All the rest of the world were fascist, Communist, or third world feudal colonies." On this interpretation, fascist countries should not be classified as "capitalistic"; private property is a necessary but not sufficient condition for classification as a "capitalistic country".

The second part of my definition of capitalism, that production be organized by and for the "market", signifies that the coordination of the activities of multiple buyers and sellers is left to acts of voluntary exchange. But the "market" is not just an abstract concept, it is also an historical process and the market, as a coordinator of economic activity, has been around for a very long time. Does this mean that the same can be said of capitalism?

For some the answer is yes – or at least the answer is that capitalism in some form has a relatively long history. Perhaps the most prominent advocates of this position are associated with "world systems theory". This approach, as its name suggests, views capitalism as always having a global character and traces a long lineage of interconnected markets and profit-making back to the Middle Ages. Capitalism, according to leading world systems theorist Immanuel Wallerstein (1979: 19), "found firm roots" in Europe with its centres in Venice and Flanders from about 1450 onwards. The trading routes which became established over the next couple of centuries between the continents all represented channels through which an economic surplus was transferred from some parts of the globe (termed the periphery) to others (termed the core), with local ruling elites taking their shares on the way as well. Thus, alliances between the beneficiaries of the process (traders, local elites, European elites) formed as various forms of surplus were appropriated by means of stealth, colonial conquest, the slave trade, taxation and trade. Thus, a "capitalist world market", with a single division of labour, became clear and was stable in form by about 1640 (Wallerstein 1979: 18). The structure of the capitalist world economy, and its division into core and periphery, dates from around this time.

This dating of a "world capitalist system" is controversial and others suggest that the economic activities described above represent part of "the long journey towards capitalism" (Beaud 2001: 41), essential for the development of capitalism but not yet constituting its "mature form". For "capitalism proper" to emerge, the development of a market for labour was required. In Europe, it took several centuries for labour to become a marketable "commodity". On this reading, capitalism is gener-ally regarded as originating in Europe, and in England more specifically, during the sixteenth to eighteenth centuries. It was during this period that changes to land ownership (the enclosure movement) led to the removal of peasants from the land and the creation of a "free" wage labour force. For the first time in history there was a class of people who were both able and required to sell their labour in the "labour market"; a "working class" had been created.

The transition to capitalism also required a change in motiva-tion so that "profit-making" became legitimate and the primary motive for entering into production. It is the profit motive that not only gives capitalism its coherence as an abstract system but also explains its dynamism through time; the many ways and changing circumstances in which profit-making takes place explain to a considerable degree how capitalism has changed over time. The necessity of making profits also explains many of the actions which capitalist firms and states have taken over time.

The profit-making motive emerged in the sixteenth to eighteenth centuries because of changes in what may be called the "enabling environment". The social environment became more conducive to the operation of markets and to the pursuit of profit-making, partly because the technological changes associated with the agricultural, and then the industrial, revolution opened up the possibilities for money-making. However, it also relied on money-making being viewed as a socially acceptable, and even desirable, activity. Here, authors such as the sociologist Max Weber (1976) attribute this change in social norms to the influence of religion, and to Protestantism in particular. According to Weber, Protestantism encouraged its followers to engage in worldly affairs and emphasized self-discipline and rationalism. This "ethic" allowed capitalism, with its emphasis on accumulation for its own sake and its restless pursuit of profit-making opportunities (or its "spirit"), to emerge. These religious changes explain why capitalism first emerged in Western Europe and North America.

To summarize, the essential elements of capitalism, as an abstract system, can be readily identified: it is a system which is based upon private property, the market and the pursuit of profit. There is more controversy, however, when we think of capitalism as a historical process, and the dating of the establishment of capitalist societies is more problematic. For some writers, the existence of markets indicates that a capitalist world system stretches back a long way, while for others the more recent emergence of labour markets suggests that capitalism "proper" emerged during the sixteenth to eighteenth centuries. Why does this matter?

It matters because this debate concerns the *scale* over which the capitalist "system" operates and how we should think about capitalism. Should we think of capitalism as a "world system"? In which case, countries which were incorporated into the "world system" – such as those in Latin America after Columbus's conquest of 1492 – can be said to have been part of the "capitalist system". Or, is capitalism primarily a nationally based "system"? In which case, we should think about capitalism primarily in national terms and view it as emerging later and spreading more slowly, and only becoming a global system in the late nineteenth/ early twentieth centuries. How we interpret today's so-called "global economy" depends very much on how we see the past.

The debate on the past has focused primarily on understanding and interpreting the transition from feudalism to capitalism in Western Europe. If we follow the argument that capitalism is a nationally based system, then more recently we have witnessed a new form of transition to capitalism – from state socialism. And in this transition, the essential elements of capitalism as an abstract system are again evident. However, in contrast to the transition from feudalism which took place over centuries, the transition to capitalism from state socialism was telescoped into a matter of years, if not months. In the countries of Eastern Europe and Russia, the enabling environment following the collapse of the Soviet bloc and facilitated by the policies of Western agencies, such as the IMF, led to the rapid establishment of capitalist societies. In Russia, for example, the "shock therapy" administered by the Russian government and the IMF in the early 1990s replaced the centrally planned socialist economy with a capitalist one within a short time period. Mass privatization schemes led to the immediate creation of a privately owned business sector. Prices were liberalized overnight so that the market would determine the prices of output and the allocation of resources. A labour market was created with the abolition of government job allocation and the reform of labour laws. The goal of profit-making was released from the social stigma which it previously attracted, and "entrepreneurship" and money-making became the new creed. The abstract requirements of a "capitalist system" were quickly put in place.

This short review has indicated that the essential elements of capitalism can be readily identified and agreed. However, the historical origins and evolution of capitalism remain contested, as the differences between world systems theorists and others on dating the emergence of capitalism have illustrated.

Identifying changes in the capitalist system over time

Capitalism is not static. How should we think about the changes in capitalism over time? One common answer is to say that first there was merchant capitalism, where the major form of capitalist activity was the trading of goods. Then there was industrial capitalism with its mass organization of the workforce into factories. This is followed by financial capitalism in which it is financial capitalists operating in banks and financial organizations whose operations dominate the economy. This periodization of capitalism – from merchant to industrial to financial capitalism, based on identifying which type of capitalist activity is dominant – is useful as a way of viewing the long-term development of capitalism.

The rise of international financial markets in the past 20 years makes financial capitalism a common descriptor of contemporary capitalism. However, the rise of "finance capital" was hotly contested at the end of the nineteenth century. One of the most famous contributors was Lenin (1948) whose *Imperialism: The Highest Stage of Capitalism* identified the merging of banks and industrial cartels as giving rise to "finance capital". It was the desire to export capital which led to the division of the globe among international monopolist firms and to European states colonizing large parts of the globe in support of their businesses. "Imperialism" was thus an advanced stage of capitalism, one relying on the rise of monopolies and on the export of capital (rather than goods), and of which colonialism was one feature. This will be discussed further as a historical process in Chapter 4.

Capitalism can also be divided between its early competitive phase and the subsequent, twentieth-century, monopoly phase driven and dominated by large corporations. Here the distinction is made not between the types of activity (trade/industry/finance) which dominate but by the nature of the market and the size and power of its competitors. Competitive capitalism describes those periods in which firms hold little market power, whereas monopoly capitalism occurs when large corporations are in control. These large corporations are typically seen as manipulating markets, through mergers and acquisitions on the supply side and through advertising on the demand side, to control the economy for their own benefit. The analysis of "monopoly capitalism" was particularly popular in Marxist circles in the 1950s and 1960s but also resonates with non-Marxist writers such as Harvard economist J.K. Galbraith. His *The New Industrial State* (1967) described the rise of a "technostructure" with its penchant for planning and control. And, of course, there are many contemporary analyses which stress the power of multinational corporations, with David Korten's (1995) analysis of the present as an era of "corporate rule" and Naomi Klein's (2000) examination of the "brand bullies" in *No Logo* being two examples. In these analyses, "corporate capitalism" is the subject of inquiry with the emphasis being on the control and power which large corporations exercise within capitalist societies.

The focus on the large corporation as a distinguishing feature of the latest phase of capitalism is also common to accounts of "modern capitalism" or "managerial capitalism". Here, however, the emphasis is not so much on the structure of the market (competitive/monopolistic) but on how, and by whom, decisions are taken. Capitalism is sometimes portrayed as having gone through an owner to a managerial phase. The rise of managers – delegated to run firms on behalf of the owners – is seen as a crucial element in the transformation of capitalism to its present-day form.

Other accounts stress the technological conditions under which capitalist production takes place and draw inferences from this about the organization of capitalist society. This type of approach is followed by the (French) Regulation school which analyses twentieth-century capitalism in terms of the movement from Fordist to post-Fordist production structures. According to this interpretation, capitalism from the 1940s and up until the end of the 1960s could be characterized as Fordist; that is, as a system of mass production – based on the techniques introduced by Henry Ford in the automobile industry. Fordist production, at least as manifested in the advanced Western countries, was combined with a welfare state, to produce a historic social agreement or accord between labour and capital. The model of capitalism which emerged was based upon a male breadwinner, kept fully employed by government policy committed to that goal. The social accord also saw workers receiving a range of social benefits in exchange for wage restraint. Income inequality was low, so that a mass market was able to provide the demand for the newly mass-produced goods.

This period gave way in the 1970s to post-Fordist production techniques based on the information and communications technology (ICT) revolution. Now, just-in-time production methods, pioneered in Japan but quickly spreading to all advanced capitalist economies, called for production methods which were "flexible" and capable of responding to changes in demand with minimum delay. The need for flexibility in production was extended to the need for flexibility in labour markets, meaning that firms had greater ability to draw upon specialist skills when required and alter levels of their workforces more frequently. This flexibility was therefore associated with "lean production" in which the number of core workers shrank and the number of part-time, casual workers increased. The power of trade unions to demarcate skill areas and negotiate employment levels was reduced, and the rewards given to the high-skilled computer whizz-kids substantially exceeded those given to the hamburger flippers. Income inequality increased as firms faced niche markets replacing mass markets. This emphasis on the technological basis of capitalist production finds further expression today in analyses of, for example, capitalism in the "information age" in which the technological requirements of ICT are shown to have altered the way work takes place and the forms that it takes.

Lastly, some have used the term "late capitalism" to describe the post-1970 period. It is "late" not in the sense of final but as distinguishing it from the capitalism of earlier periods. This approach relies on the same changes in the production process described by the Regulation school – the emergence of "a world capitalist system fundamentally distinct from the older imperialism" (Jameson 1991: xix) under the auspices of the multinational corporation, the ICT revolution and the new forms of labour flexibility. One of the distinguishing features of late capitalism is that it has produced its own "postmodern" culture in which "culture" itself has become "marketized" or "commodified".

Late capitalism is characterized by the triumph of image over substance, of spin over policy, of rampant consumerism and of the "commodification" of objects as well as human subjects. Andy Warhol's famous paintings of Marilyn Monroe are held up as a prominent example of postmodern art. The individual is fragmented and multi-imaged, reflecting the fragmented and multi-tasked features of production in late capitalism.[5]

All of these categories, summarized in Box 1.3, point to the fact that while capitalism has essential constant features, it has also changed considerably over time. Capitalism is at once a conceptual system and at the same time a dynamic historical process. The periodization of capitalism into the various phases discussed in this chapter represent different ways of emphasizing some of the more important changes that have taken place over time. In Chapters 4–7, I will return to these themes and discuss how capitalism has varied over time and space in the twentieth century. In Chapters 4, 5 and 6, in particular, the approach I will take is based on the proposition that capitalism is best analysed in its national contexts; the foregoing discussion

BOX 1.3

Ways of looking at capitalism over time

1   By dominant activity – from *merchant* to *industrial* to *financial* capitalism.

2   By the nature of the market – from *competitive* to *monopoly* capitalism.

3   By firm ownership – from *owner* to *managerial* capitalism.

4   By technology and social regulation – mass production (*Fordism*) to flexible production (*post-Fordism*).

5   By technology and culture – mass production (*modern*) to consumerist late capitalism (*postmodern*).

should alert the reader to the fact that this is not an uncontested proposition.

Before analysing further the historical process, in Chapters 2 and 3 I will consider capitalism at the abstract and normative levels: just what does an economic and social system based on the institutions of private property, the market and the profit motive mean for us?

Further reading

For those interested in a short overview of the history of capitalism and some of the debates surrounding it, Michel Beaud's, *A History of Capitalism 1500–2000*, New York: Monthly Review Press, fifth edition, 2001 is a brilliant starting point. The world systems perspective can be found in Immanuel Wallerstein's essay "The rise and future demise of the world capitalist system:

Concepts of comparative analysis" in his edited collection *The Capitalist World Economy*, Cambridge: Cambridge University Press, 1979.

The links between religion and the rise of capitalism were explored by Ralph Tawney in his classic *Religion and the Rise of Capitalism: A Historical Study*, Harmondsworth: Penguin, 1984, as well as by Weber (1976). Religious and/or cultural explanations for capitalism's emergence and growth have also been common more recently, only now it has been the "Confucian" ethic for hard work – rather than the "Protestant ethic" – that has been the centre of attention and that has been used to help explain the rise of Japan and other East Asian countries in the past half century. See, for example, the essays exploring this issue in Tai Hung-chao's edited collection, *Confucianism and Economic Development: An Oriental Alternative?*, Washington DC: Washington Institute Press, 1989. Whether these religious and cultural explanations for capitalism's emergence and growth are really satisfactory is open to doubt; why, for example, was the influence of Confucianism important after, say, 1960 in Taiwan and South Korea but not before?

For a contribution by the Regulation school see, for example, Alain Lipietz, *Towards a New Economic Order: Postfordism, Ecology and Democracy*, New York: Oxford University Press, 1992. For the postmodern analysis of late capitalism, Frederic Jameson's *Postmodernism, Or the Cultural Logic of Late Capitalism*, Durham: Duke University Press, 1991, is a superb, but at times difficult, book. For Marxist analysis of the stage of monopoly capitalism, a classic work here is Paul Baran and Paul Sweezy, *Monopoly Capital: An Essay on the American Economic and Social Order*, Harmondsworth: Penguin, 1968.

Notes

1 Robbins (2002: 14) notes that "by 1998, the amount spent globally on advertising reached $437 billion, a figure that rivals the $778 billion spent on weapons".

2 See, for example, Heilbroner (1985), McQueen (2001) and de Soto (2000) respectively.

3 On Russia see Klebnikov (2001), on "crony capitalism" see Kang (2002) and Haber (2002), and on Angola see Hodges (2001). On "digital capitalism", see Schiller (1999).

4 There has been much discussion of the way in which capitalism operates in this way and can be illustrated with the example of Christmas. As Robbins (2002: 24) explains: "Santa Claus represents one of the more elaborate ways in which the culture of capitalism shields its members, particularly children, from some of its less savoury features. The story of Santa Claus represented a world in which consumer, capitalist, and labourer were idealized: Commodities (toys) were manufactured by happy elves, working in Santa's workshops (no factories at the North Pole, and certainly no Chinese assembly plants) and distributed, free of charge, to good boys and girls by a corpulent, grandfatherly male in fur-trimmed clothes."

5 See Jameson (1991) for more on this.

CHAPTER 2

Capitalism as a system: "natural" and "free"

Introduction

ON A TRIP TO AUSTRALIA in November 2002, US Trade Representative Robert Zoellick stated that "free trade is about freedom".[1] His remark was intended to highlight the values of "openness" and "freedom", values that "terrorists are trying to destroy". By linking together free trade – the unrestricted movement of goods and operation of markets – with freedom, Zoellick was using for contemporary purposes a long-standing claim made by supporters of capitalism. The claim is that capitalism means freedom and global capitalism will bring global freedom. Why and how such a claim is made is set out in this chapter.

Advocates of "free market" capitalism regard it as a system, at the abstract level, which is "natural" and which constitutes an integral part of human "freedom". The interpretation of the market, one of the fundamental defining characteristics of capitalism, as a site of freedom, and upon which Zoellick drew, can readily be traced back to eigtheenth-century writer Adam Smith (1976), widely regarded as the founder of the discipline of economics and best known for his support of a free market system (Box 2.1).

BOX 2.1

Adam Smith: 1723–1790

Adam Smith, born in Scotland, is often invoked as the source of ideas about the beneficial workings of the market. He was a Professor of Moral Philosophy at the University of Glasgow when he wrote his most famous book, *An Inquiry into the Nature and Causes of the Wealth of Nations*. Published in 1776, the book is widely viewed as a free market manifesto.

The book argues that an economic system based on competitive markets is best suited to human nature and provides the best route to material advancement. The market should be used wherever possible. Smith not only advocated free trade but also the payment of teachers by the popularity of their classes. Competition, for Smith, was always necessary – even among religions. Unregulated markets were the best way to provide this competition. Government restrictions on markets should be limited to a few special cases.

While Smith's pro-market views have become widely known, he was actually a bit more complicated. He also wrote a book entitled *The Theory of Moral Sentiments* (1759) which argued that fellow-feeling, rather than self-interest, was a dominant human trait. In the *Wealth of Nations* he argued that no society could be happy if the bulk of the population did not share in its prosperity, and he viewed business people as frequently seeking to take advantage of consumers. Ironically, given his views on free trade and taxes, he ended his life working for the Board of Customs in Edinburgh.

Adam Smith: markets are natural for humans . . . but not for dogs

The act of market exchange was, for Smith, "natural" in the sense that it was based upon a propensity which was found in all humans and, more strongly, only in humans. That is, for Smith, market exchange was a central defining characteristic of our own humanness. The question "what distinguishes humans as humans?" was a well-debated topic at the end of the eighteenth century. For some, the answer to this lay in the ability of humans to communicate and to develop language. For Smith, the answer was to be found in humans' ability to enter into exchange.

Smith (1976: 25) refers to this as "the propensity to truck, barter and exchange", in other words, to trade. This propensity, Smith (1976: 25–26) tells us, "is common to all men, and to be found in no other race of animals, which seem to know neither this nor any other species of contracts. Two greyhounds, in running down the same hare, have sometimes the appearance of acting in some sort of concert. Each turns her towards his companion, or endeavors to intercept her when his companion turns her towards himself. This, however, is not the effect of any contract, but of the accidental concurrence of their passions in the same object at that particular time. Nobody ever saw a dog make a fair and deliberate exchange of one bone for another with another dog. Nobody ever saw one animal by its gestures and natural cries signify to another, this is mine, that yours; I am willing to give this for that."

From this view, important implications arise. Firstly, market exchange, being based on a natural propensity, is common to all people and all places. The "market" is a universal institution arising from an innate "propensity" within human beings. Attempts to limit exchange are regarded as both futile and oppressive. They are futile in that they attempt to deny human nature and, as such, will ultimately fail. Thus, attempts to limit the operations of the market in many countries, such as those which occurred in the countries of the former communist bloc, simply resulted in the rise of "black" or "grey" market activity; that is, in market exchange which was not officially sanctioned by the state. Attempts to suppress the market in any significant degree could not work in the long run, since human nature would always find an avenue to escape the shackles of any state-imposed restrictions. The contemporary relevance of this view is not only that economic systems which seek to radically limit the operations of the market are doomed to failure because human ingenuity, propelled by the "propensity to truck, barter, and exchange", will overcome such limitations. This position also implies that the transition to a market system can be achieved reasonably quickly, since markets will "naturally" and spontaneously develop. For example, the "transition to capitalism" in the former Soviet bloc could possibly be a short one if a supportive enabling environment was quickly established.

The second implication of Smith's argument is that limits on market exchange are limits on human freedom. If our humanity is expressed and defined by our ability to enter into exchange relationships with others, then any attempts to limit these exchanges are therefore attempts to limit our humanity.

This implication was taken up more fully in the works of Chicago, and Nobel Prize-winning, economist Milton Friedman (Box 2.2).

BOX 2.2

Milton Friedman: born 1912

Milton Friedman's best-known contribution is as a "monetarist". According to this theory, governments cannot permanently reduce unemployment by intervening in the economy. All they are likely to do is to cause inflation. Governments should therefore focus on controlling inflation; once they have done this, competitive markets will bring about full employment. This view, known as "The Chicago School" view after the name of the University where Friedman taught for 30 years, was influential around the world, especially in the 1970s and 1980s. Friedman's contributions led to the award of the Nobel Prize in Economics in 1976.

Friedman has also been a tireless advocate of capitalism as the best economic system. His two most famous books on the subject, co-authored with Rose Friedman, are *Capitalism and Freedom* (1962) and *Free to Choose* (1980). They argue that market capitalism promotes human freedom and that government interventions to promote equality – through rent controls and minimum wages, for example – produce less equitable outcomes than market processes as well as infringing upon freedom.

Milton Friedman on markets, freedom and Alka Seltzer

Individuals in a market system are, in the Friedmans' words, "free to choose". And the more areas over which choice can be made, the freer we are as individuals. Government interventions in the market are seen as restricting freedom. As the Friedmans argued, "a citizen of the United States who under the laws of various states is not free to follow the occupation of his own choosing unless he can get a license for it, is . . . being deprived of an essential part of his freedom. So is the man who would like to exchange some of his goods with, say, a Swiss for a watch but is prevented from doing so by a quota. So also is the Californian who was thrown in jail for selling Alka Seltzer at a price below that set the manufacturer under so-called "fair trade" laws. So also is the farmer who cannot grow the amount of wheat he wants. And so on." (1962: 9) As a general rule, therefore, any exchange which is voluntary and informed should be permitted to take place; if it is not, it is limiting our freedom.

This position, that free markets constitute human freedom and that all forms of voluntary exchange should not only be tolerated but encouraged, has found resonance in many policies introduced by conservative governments throughout the world. For example, the assault on the welfare state under the Thatcher government in the UK was as much an assault at the ideological level, based on the freedom-enhancing claims of "the market", as it was because of inherent problems of the welfare state.[2] Part of the argument against the welfare state was that it unfairly restricted the ability of individuals to purchase goods (especially in the areas of health and education). Freedom was thereby reduced.

Are there exceptions to this rule? If "goods" such as pornography, guns, drugs, human organs, private armies and weapons of mass destruction are not freely available for sale, is freedom reduced? Advocates of the "free market" have had difficulty with this question. In theory, the libertarian tradition points to wider rather than restricted markets. In practice, all capitalist societies have had to struggle with the question of whether unrestricted markets should be permitted or whether a public interest, over and above the market, should be invoked. For example, the market for guns varies by country, and various regulations determine which guns and which owners are legal. Drugs have varied through time in their legality, as has pornography.[3]

More from Adam Smith: markets feed us because of self-interest

A third implication of Smith's analysis is that the motive for entering into exchange is self-interest. I enter into exchange because I value more highly that which I can obtain from you than that which I currently possess, and vice versa. Exchange is therefore based upon self-interest. This is summed up in Smith's (1976: 26–27) famous statement that "it is not from the benevolence of the butcher, the brewer, or the baker, that we expect our dinner, but from their regard to their own interest". That is, the baker does not sell me bread because s/he wants to remove my hunger but because s/he wishes to make a profit. Market interactions, which have increasingly dominated human interactions, are based on self-interest. A society which functions on the basis of self-interest might be regarded as anything from slightly unseemly to downright immoral and inhuman. For Smith, and subsequent supporters of capitalism, however, it is no such thing; it arises from human propensities and many benefits spring from it. The profit motive is "natural".

For Smith, the propensity to exchange (based on self-interest) permitted the division of labour – because I am willing to enter into exchange, I do not need to produce all that I need but can specialize and exchange my surplus production for yours. And it was this specialization and division of labour which allowed countries to greatly increase their productivity and to raise general living standards. Furthermore, the self-interested actions of individuals produced the growth that benefited all: the "Invisible Hand" at work. The "Invisible Hand" metaphor used by Smith is a very powerful one; it is based on the argument that the self-interested actions of individuals lead, not to chaos, but to order and to socially desirable outcomes. Prosperity and social progress is brought about, not by the deliberate interventions of policy-makers seeking to promote social welfare, but as the unintended outcome of decentralized decisions driven by self-interest.

This analysis leads to a simple but powerful conclusion: capitalism is a system capable of maximizing social welfare while minimizing government intervention. If the market is left to operate freely then this will lead to better, albeit unintended, social outcomes than even the best-intentioned interventions of governments seeking to impose their preferred outcomes. And government interventions are often very far from best-intentioned. This conclusion, of the social welfare maximizing properties of markets, relies on these markets being competitive markets. It is not surprising that writers such as the Friedmans (1962) attribute monopolies to restrictions placed upon the market by governments rather than by the workings of the market itself. In the absence of government ownership and government restrictions, capitalist markets are presumed to be overwhelmingly competitive.

Smith, Friedman and their followers believe that markets and profit-making are "natural". Furthermore, the operation of markets constitutes an important component of human freedom. But is self-interest enough to keep society together? Where do "values" come from? For some of capitalism's supporters, self-interest is sufficient and individual preferences and values are seen as innate. For others, "values" need to be reinforced by non-market moral compasses provided by religious and/or "family" values, for example. Politically, these differences are expressed in contemporary societies in the tensions between the libertarian and the socially conservative Right. Both are pro-capitalist, but they differ on the need for extra-market social institutions to guide human behaviour. In the market sphere, however, both sides agree that self-interest is natural and desirable.

Is private property "natural" as well?

Smith's previously cited quotation (1976: 25–26) implies the strict linkage of markets with private property. His statement "this is mine, that yours" implies that goods are owned by individuals. Markets and private property go together. However, this is a much more difficult position to sustain historically; and the philosophical or moral case for private property is difficult to sustain as well.

Private property can be defended on the basis of its justness and/or its utility. In terms of its justness, there is a well-established argument that individuals should, morally, own the fruits of their own labour. John Locke, for example, writing in the late 1600s argued (1960: 328) that, with respect to an individual, "the labour of his body, and the work of his hands we may say, are properly his". Likewise, Smith (1976: 138) argued that "the property which every man has in his own labour, as it is the original foundation of all other property, so it is the most sacred and inviolable". Present-day arguments that the creators of knowledge/products/processes deserve to be protected through intellectual property rights rely on essentially the same appeal.

The utility of private property typically rests on the argument that private property, as an institution, has shown itself to support the market system and that this has proved to be the most effective way of raising general living standards. The stronger version of this is that private property has proven itself *necessary* to support the market system. This necessity relies on the proposition that in order to be an entrepreneur, a risk-taker, the shaker and mover of the capitalist system, individuals must be secure in the knowledge that they will enjoy the benefits of their entrepreneurship or risk-taking. Such security can only be provided by the right to private property.[4]

Private property can be supported, therefore, on the grounds of its justness and of its utility. Nevertheless, upholding private property rights remains controversial in some circumstances. For example, in the name of private property, homeless people are evicted from unoccupied, but privately owned, buildings. Teenagers may not copy music but, since life itself can be owned, scientists can copy (clone) a sheep. Countries which at some point in their histories underwent revolutions are not admitted back into international forums until they have agreed to pay for any "illegally" seized assets. Furthermore, whatever the merit of the justness and utility claims, the rise of private property as empirical matter, that is *historically*, has seldom, if ever, been the result of such theoretical niceties; force and theft have been the historical rule by which rights to private property have been established.

The problematic defence of the institution of private property has meant that, as an ideology, "the market" or "the free market"

have often been used as metaphors for capitalism. This con-
veniently neglects private property, the other essential pillar
of capitalism. The right to private property as an overriding,
uninfringeable, right is much harder to sell than the notion that
"the market" should be allowed to operate as it offers freedom
of choice to consumers.[5] Proponents are therefore typically
much more comfortable defending the "free market" economy
than the "private property" economy.

The state as impartial rule enforcer

The protection of private property gives rise to the need for the
state. Otherwise, there would be something of a dilemma here:
if capitalism is natural, and government intervention so bad, why
is a state needed? One way to give a clear answer to this is with
the use of a sporting analogy. In a chapter on the "free market"
economy and entitled "The only natural economy", Stanford
University's John McMillan (2002: 13) argues that "a typical
market is born and grows like football. It evolves spontaneously,
driven by its participants. It can operate with little or no formal
structure – but only up to a point. To reach a degree of sophistica-
tion, its procedures need to be clarified and an authority given
the power to enforce them. Only when the informal rules are
supplemented by some formal rules can a market reach its
full potential, with transactions being conducted efficiently and
complex dealings being feasible. An absolutely free market is
like folk football, a free-for-all brawl. A real market is like
American football, an ordered brawl."

The American football analogy highlights a number of
points. Capitalist markets are seen as natural and as arising

"spontaneously". However, the state is needed after a certain point to enable capitalism to flourish because rules, and an enforcer of those rules, is needed. This is the role that the state should play under capitalism: as an enforcer of the rules of private property. The state is part of the game but is not an active player; rather the state plays the role of referee, ensuring that there is fair competition between the contestants. The football analogy also sums up an important claim for capitalism: whoever wins does so because of a combination of good skill, hard work and good luck. These are the attributes which are rewarded under capitalism – not class privilege, for example.[6] The state is therefore a neutral referee of a fair competitive game, although its function is also to ensure that it is football that is being played and that one side does not suddenly decide that cricket would be more to its liking and force the other side to play that.

This provides a minimal but absolutely essential role for the state to play. To the defence of private property, through contract enforcement, we should also add national defence. As the Friedmans (1962: 2) argue, "the scope of government must be limited. Its major function must be to protect our freedom both from the enemies outside our gates and from our fellow-citizens: to preserve law and order to enforce voluntary contracts, to foster competitive markets".

Some states are better rule enforcers than others – and so sometimes capitalism fails

The importance of a state-run, well-functioning legal system is therefore critical to the successful operation of a capitalist system. Indeed, Hernando de Soto (2000), working at the Institute for Liberty and Democracy in Peru, has argued that it is the ability of Western societies to develop well-established and widely respected legal systems for the enforcement of contracts and the protection of private property that has led capitalism in the West to be so successful but a failure in the rest of the world. It is the absence of domestic legal structures and *mores* in the developing world that explains why capitalism has failed to produce there the standards of living that are enjoyed in the West. The vast majority of the poor, he argues, have assets but these assets are unable to form the basis of a successful capitalist economy because of the absence of a functioning legal framework; the capitalist system includes a set of norms and rules which enable it to function effectively.

Advocates of capitalism argue that it is both natural and free. However, a state is needed to act as the referee, the enforcer of the rules of the game, rather than as an active participant making the plays.

Capitalism is also the most economically productive system

Implicit in much of the argument so far of the philosophical justification of capitalism as an abstract system, is the argument that such a system also happens to be economically desirable. That is, to the philosophical argument that capitalism is capable of delivering human freedom must be added a pragmatic argument that capitalism is a system which is not only capable of, but is also the best suited to, delivering material benefits. This pragmatic argument receives wider support and is accepted by many as the justification for capitalism, even if they do not embrace the philosophical arguments with enthusiasm.

As a practical matter, it is argued that the capitalist market system best solves the "coordination problem" and, secondly, that it best provides the incentives for innovation and techno-logical progress. The coordination problem is simply this: how can the production and consumption decisions of millions of agents be organized so that the outcome is desirable rather than chaotic? The coordination problem is resolved in capitalism by the use of markets. Markets – the interactions of buyers and sellers – determine prices which permit goods to be sold for all those willing to offer their goods for sale at the market price and all purchasers willing to pay the market price to buy the goods. In this way, markets, by establishing prices, allow voluntary exchange to coordinate the economy.

Central to the claim that this process is desirable, in the sense that it solves the problem well, is the proposition that markets lead to equilibrium. That is, both individual markets and the economy as a whole have a tendency to equilibrium. Capitalist markets are seen as robust and self-adjusting; equilibrium can be expected if the market is allowed to operate freely. Disequilibrium in individual markets – meaning an imbalance between supply and demand – is restored through a change in price. This may be obvious in the case of many goods. However, Friedman (1953) also famously argued that the same mechanism can be relied upon in markets, such as the foreign exchange market, where fluctuations are often the norm. In such cases, the price mechanism should again be allowed to work and the actions of speculators are argued, in general, to be "stabilizing rather than the reverse" (1953: 175).

The main problems which arise at the level of the economy as a whole – inflation and unemployment, for example – are viewed as being primarily the result of destabilizing government policies: excess money creation in the case of inflation, and institutional frictions such as minimum wages and pro-trade union bargaining legislation in the case of unemployment. Provided that governments adhere to strict monetary discipline and encourage flexibility in all other markets, the capitalist system can be expected to perform well. This has been the central policy position of proponents of capitalism and has been enshrined in the policy advice given by international organizations, such as the IMF and the World Bank, to all comers. The basic argument here is that the capitalist system is inherently self-adjusting and stable.

For much of the early post-1945 period, capitalism's claim to solve the coordination problem more efficiently than other economic systems looked suspect as the Soviet Union posted impressive growth rates and seemed to be catching up with the West. Here, planners solved the coordination problem. Government officials, armed with input–output tables, sought to track and organize the flow of goods and services through the economy. As long as computers could be made powerful enough, the planners argued, the increasing complexity of the economy could be handled. As it happened, it could not be handled and the demise of the centrally planned system from the mid-1980s onwards led to the reassertion that only the market could solve the coordination problem in complex economies. Planning proved to be unable to ensure that, for example, the desired number of size 4, red shoes with white laces was available in stores across the country. Only the decentralized market, equipped with profit incentives, could ensure that it was in everyone's self-interest that this was achieved. In fact, the centrally planned system often found it difficult to ensure that basic goods such as bread and meat were available, let alone the latest styles in fashion footwear.

Only capitalism produces the goods people want, it is argued. Furthermore, if the objective of production is to maximize profits, then it is in producers' interests to use the lowest cost combination of inputs and to use them as efficiently as possible. Allocating inputs as well as final goods was therefore best coordinated by the millions of individual decisions of producers and consumers rather than attempted by the supposedly all-knowing economic bureaucracy which characterized state socialism.

The second part of the claim that capitalism is a superior economic system in terms of its ability to produce goods for the mass of the population rests on its capacity for innovation. That is, the production of new goods, and of new ways of producing existing goods, requires an incentive. Capitalism provides this through the existence of private profits and encourages "entrepreneurial spirit" in individuals.

Capitalism – the most economically productive system and therefore the "end of history"

These economic strengths of the capitalist system are argued by writers such as Fukuyama (1992) to demonstrate that capitalism is likely to be the preferred system of economic organization for all countries, both for advanced industrial (or core or developed) countries and for developing (or Third World) countries. And, as a result, the capitalist economy is the "end of history" in the sense that the major economic problems are solved with this type of economy. Although some improvements can always be made, they do not involve a change of system (Box 2.3).

In arguing for this controversial thesis, Fukuyama (1992) appeals to many of the arguments presented above. Material

BOX 2.3

Francis Fukuyama: born 1952

Propelled to the status of international guru as a result of a 1989 article "The end of history", Fukuyama argued that communism was finished and that Western liberal capitalism had won the Cold War. The book that was written on the same subject, *The End of History and the Last Man* (1992), was an international best-seller and appeared in 20 foreign editions. Its story – that capitalism had won and that there would be no more changes to the social system – caught the triumphalist mood of capitalism perfectly.

The argument relied on a reading of human nature – of what history had shown that humans wanted. In a subsequent book, Fukuyama argued that capitalism also needed people to develop high levels of "trust" for capitalism to achieve its potential. In another recent book, entitled *Our Posthuman Future: Consequences of the Biotechnology Revolution* (2002), he argues that biotechnology may undermine society, since the possibilities for human cloning now threaten the existence of "human nature". Fukuyama supports an international ban on human cloning, even if voluntary exchange would otherwise occur. Without a ban, one of the assumptions of liberal democracy, that every individual is born equal, would be violated. McMillan's "ordered brawl" would be unfair if one team was a genetically engineered "super-race". Fukuyama's latest work illustrates some of the problems that even the most ardent pro-capitalist supporters have in justifying the "rule of the market" in all cases.

advancement is driven by technology – "modern natural science" in Fukuyama's words. Humans have shown themselves to desire greater material well-being and, despite sporadic attempts to limit or even reject technological progress and material advance, the general historical trend and the preference of the majority of the world's population has been for increased material well-being and technological change. Modern industrial societies require the coordination of millions of individuals and the setting of billions of market prices. While the centrally planned Soviet-style system was able to perform well when faced with a primitive industrial economy, it proved itself unable to cope with the complex demands of the types of post-industrial economies which exist in present-day advanced countries. Neither could its centralized system generate the levels of technology and innovation that the decentralized, free market system could, with its set of incentives and its absence of constraints. It is only the decentralized, capitalist market mechanism that has proved capable of doing this. Capitalism, therefore, will emerge as the dominant system for advanced countries. As Fukuyama argues (1992: 96–97), "the unfolding of technologically driven economic modernization creates strong incentives for developed countries to accept the basic terms of the universal capitalist culture, by permitting a substantial degree of economic competition and letting prices be determined by market mechanisms. No other path toward full economic modernity has proven to be viable."

In developing countries, less concerned with the complexities posed in advanced economies and more concerned with achieving a structural change in the economy towards industry, it might be thought that the state and economic planning would play a larger role. However, here Fukuyama again appeals to the empirical evidence and argues that the economic success of East Asian countries such as Singapore, Hong Kong, Thailand, South Korea and Malaysia – some of the countries of the so-called "East Asian miracle" – prove that capitalism is the best system for achieving economic advancement in developing countries. Here, according to Fukuyama's interpretation, countries with few natural resources and whose only initial economic advantage was an abundant supply of relatively well-educated, low-paid workers, have seen dramatic increases in living standards as a result of freeing markets and integrating into the global capitalist economy. On this interpretation of the East Asian experience, what developing countries need is more, not less, capitalism.[7]

This reasoning leads Fukuyama to foresee "the creation of a universal consumer culture based on liberal economic principles, for the Third World as well as the First and the Second. The enormously productive and dynamic economic world created by advancing technology and the rational organization of labour has a tremendous homogenizing power. It is capable of linking different societies around the world to one another physically through the creation of global markets, and of creating parallel economic aspirations and practices in a host of diverse societies. The attractive power of this world creates a very strong *predisposition* for all human societies to participate in it, while success in this participation requires the adoption of the principles of economic liberalism" (1992: 108).

All peoples and countries are driven to capitalism; it represents the end point of the human struggle for material advancement. But if capitalism, based on the institutions of the market and private property, and motivated by the desire for profits, is here to stay as Fukuyama suggests, and if this provides us with an essential component of human freedom, what else can we expect? What does capitalism, defined as a form of economic organization in this way, imply about the political sphere, about social justice, about the environment? What can be deduced, if anything, about the wider characteristics of the capitalist system?

Does capitalism lead to democracy?

Does capitalism, as an economic form of organization, lead to specific political forms of organization? This question has usually been asked in terms of the relationship between capitalism and democracy; in short, does the economic freedom attributed to capitalism also translate to political freedom in the form of democracy?

When framing this question, political freedom is usually defined as the ability to hold any political views without prejudice (provided that they do not do injury to others), to free association, and to vote. The relationship between capitalism and democracy has typically been premised on this definition of political freedom. It should be noted, however, that "democracy" is a contested term and is capable of being defined in a number of ways. The definition of political freedom provided above, and incorporating democratic elections, is typically referred to as procedural or representative democracy. Substantive democracy, however, refers to a wider set of practices, including social rights (for genders, groups and classes), which translate into an equitable distribution of wealth and opportunities. This definition of democracy may also include the exercise of democracy in the workplace (or economic democracy). Typically, substantive and economic democracy are not the topics of analysis, and the relationship between capitalism and representative democracy has occupied the bulk of debate.

Historically, capitalism has coexisted with a variety of political forms. It has coexisted with authoritarian regimes in much of the developing world (witness Pinochet's Chile, for example), with absolute monarchies (witness the Saudi Arabian oil kingdom, for example), with fascist regimes (if one is willing to include them as capitalist countries as discussed in Chapter 1), and with procedural or representative democracies. Given this array of political forms found in capitalist countries, an association between economic form and political form would seem to be unlikely.

Despite this, it is frequently asserted that capitalism and democracy go together. Why? One explanation is based on two empirical regularities: firstly, that the advanced capitalist countries tend to have political systems which are based upon procedural/representative democracy (and, indeed, all 24 current members of the OECD are characterized in this way) and thus economic growth might be expected to produce democracy. Secondly, representative democracies, in the modern era, have been established only in capitalist societies.

The association between capitalism and democracy is also partly based on the theoretical proposition that dispersed economic power, in the form of millions of individual economic agents, is the best bulwark against the possibility of governments abusing their power (see the Friedmans 1962). If governments are large, they are able to impose their views on the majority by threatening to withhold means of livelihoods (or worse) and thereby coerce individuals. When governments become all-encompassing, they become totalitarian states. The market provides alternative means of livelihood for individuals and thereby enables them to retain their political independence. To allow government to take a larger role is, in Friedrich von Hayek's (1944) language, the "road to serfdom". The choice Hayek (Box 2.4) offers us is between totalitarian serfdom and capitalist liberty.

BOX 2.4

Friedrich von Hayek: 1899–1992

Born in Austria, Friedrich von Hayek developed the view that society and the economy are complex evolutionary systems. As such, they cannot, except at great cost, be "planned". The "fatal conceit" of socialist and totalitarian regimes is to believe that they can consciously plan society and the economy. They offer human-designed utopias but end up delivering only human-imposed "serfdom".

Individuals are at the centre of Hayek's work. Each individual makes plans and has knowledge and information. The knowledge and information which individuals and firms in the economy possess can best be utilized in a free market capitalist economy. Only here will prices be established in markets which best reflect the preferences of millions (and billions) of consumers and firms. Central ministries simply cannot know all of the information needed to run an economy and inefficiency is bound to result in government-run economies. Decentralized systems with individuals free to express their preferences best solve the coordination problem.

More broadly, individuals are best able to realize their potential as human beings when they are free to express their thoughts and preferences in "open societies", that is, societies in which governments are constrained and individual liberty is guaranteed. Hayek's *The Constitution of Liberty* (1960) sets out the principles for how such a society could be governed.

This argument suggests simply that capitalist economies are necessary for the exercise of political democracy. Can a stronger case be made, namely, that there are historical forces at work which make capitalism a sufficient condition for the establishment of democracy?

In this context, a special role has been assigned to the middle class. The central proposition is that if a property-owning, trading middle class emerges then its interest will be for the expansion of the market and the non-arbitrary exercise of power. That is, a functioning capitalist market system requires the "rule of law" rather than the "rule of men". The wealth and influence of the middle class will eventually lead to the transition to a system (a number of means are possible, violent and non-violent) in which the rule of law and checks and balances on the arbitrary exercise of power through representative assemblies is established. This argument has been put to the test recently following the spectacular growth in East and Southeast Asian countries since 1960. The issue is whether the emerging middle class has been the driving force towards political liberalization in these countries. The counter-argument is that the middle classes of the successful Asian countries have not been interested in wider systemic political change but have been happy to accept a more inclusive form of authoritarianism in which their interests have been recognized and served. Certainly, capitalism in these countries has brought some political realignment, but it is by no means clear that genuine democracies have been the outcome.

The proposition that a prosperous middle class will be a force for democratic change nevertheless holds sway in many quarters and not only provides a historical account of how capitalism led to political freedoms but also provides a guide to foreign policy.

That is, it is frequently advocated that increasing trade with, for example, communist China or revolutionary Iran is the best way of fostering democratization in those countries. By supporting the emergence and consolidation of a middle class through trade, it is hoped that the process of democratization will be advanced.

Others are more sceptical of a causal relationship. For example, Fukuyama, who regarded the capitalist economy as the "end of history", argued that this historical end point would be accompanied by liberal (or representative) democracy. But there is no causal connection between the two. On this, Fukuyama is clear: "there is no economically necessary reason why advanced industrialization should produce political liberty" (1992: xv).

Fukuyama does not believe that capitalism causes political liberty. Instead, it is a separate force, the desire for recognition, that brings about political liberty. He argues that all political systems which do not recognize citizens as equals lack the legitimacy which will enable them to endure. Eventually, they will be replaced by a political system that duly accords equality to all – and representative democracy with equal rights for all citizens is the only system that can provide this in the modern world. For Fukuyama, this is the lesson of the past 200 years as the scope of political liberty has, as a long-run trend, increased around the world.

Indeed, there has been a long-run upward trend in the proportion of the world's population living in democratic societies. The 1990s marked a milestone in this respect with over half of the world's countries being "democracies" – a historical first.[8] The democratic content of much of the "democratic transition" of the 1990s is certainly open to doubt. In some cases, elections have demonstrably been neither free nor fair (for example,

Zimbabwe), in others political leaders have been found guilty of corruption (for example, Mexico and South Korea) and in others the military have quickly reversed the trend (for example, Peru and Pakistan). Nevertheless, the relationship between economic growth, globalization and democracy continues to be the subject of enquiry. However, regardless of any correlations, it is unclear whether this is underpinned by a causal relationship between capitalism and democracy as the above discussion illustrates. The argument that "capitalism brings political freedom" remains unproved.

Capitalism as equal and just

Can we expect capitalist societies to be "equal" and "just"? Its advocates portray capitalism as the triumph of the individual. The individuals in this account are not gendered or differentiated by race, religion or, for that matter, time. That is, capitalism is seen as a system equally appropriate to all people and all times. Each individual can, and indeed wishes to, advance their material interests and claim their individual freedom by participating voluntarily in the capitalist market system. Each person has an equal right to that freedom; equality here is equality to participate in the market. A further claim is that a competitive capitalist market is, to use Hayek's (1944) word, "blind". That is, when we buy goods we do not know who made them; we are unable to discriminate on the basis of our prejudices and, as a result, the market system is capable of delivering a non-discriminatory society in which many beliefs can be held because the means of discriminating between people are absent in the "blind" market process. The market, in the views of the Friedmans (1962) and fellow conservatives, is the friend of "minorities" and their best defence against discrimination.

Economically, capitalism is most unlikely to lead to equal, or even roughly equal, levels of income. It is not equality of outcomes that capitalism offers. If redress is desired then taxation is necessary. However, the more strident advocates of liberal capitalism have argued that this should be limited. In their view poverty alleviation, where poverty is narrowly defined, may be a legitimate function of government but income redistribution is not. This is because to redistribute income is to seek an equality of outcomes which infringes upon the rights of individuals to the fruits of their labour (a justification for private property which goes back to Locke in the seventeenth century). If incomes are unequally distributed then this is because some individuals work harder and/or consumers value their services more highly than those of others. Thus, to protect the right to earn the fruits of one's own labour and to permit the allocative function of a labour market, inequalities in outcomes should be regarded as both just and necessary.

If taxation is required, then a case has been made for proportional rather than progressive taxation.[9] This case relies again on a combination of moral and practical reasons. The moral reason is that it is unjust for a majority to impose rates of taxation on a minority which it is unwilling to bear itself. In Hayek's (1960) view, this is precisely what progressive taxation does. The practical arguments are that high rates of taxation discourage work by the most productive members of the economy and act as a restraint on entrepreneurship.

These arguments, while largely regarded as ill-founded, and even extreme, in the advanced capitalist countries in the decades

after 1945, have recently found more resonance as a more conservative ideology has taken hold. For example, rates of taxation
on high income earners have been cut substantially in many of
the advanced capitalist economies in order, it is argued, to provide incentives for the rich to work harder. There have been proposals in some countries for "flat taxes", i.e. for a proportional
income tax rate (and even for lump sum taxes, such as the UK
tried with a poll tax). Certainly, the direction in which taxes have
been moving in the advanced capitalist countries since the mid-
1980s has been away from progressive income taxes and towards
more regressive sales taxes (like GST and VAT) where the poor
pay higher proportions of their incomes in taxes than the rich.
Such a trend has been promoted as both desirable and necessary
for the improvement of the workings of the capitalist system.

Capitalism as a friend of the environment

Proponents argue that capitalism, and the latest phase, global
capitalism, will contribute to meeting environmental objectives.
The argument is that capitalism, being a profit-motivated system, will ensure that goods are produced using the minimum
level of inputs necessary. This includes minimizing the use of
natural resources. Free trade and environmental sustainability
are compatible goals on this reading; if production can be organized globally then this will lead to increased "efficiency" in the
use of natural resources, as they will be sourced from where they
are most abundant, a relative abundance which will be reflected
in a lower price. Enabling firms to seek resources on the global
market will lead to their being conserved in places where they
are scarce.

One of the main environmental problems, the "tragedy of the commons", is caused, according to proponents of capitalism, precisely by the absence of private property and the market. The "tragedy of the commons" refers to tragedies such as the depletion of fish stocks and of the ozone layer. They are tragedies because these resources are treated as "commons", that is, owned by everyone and so not really owned by anyone. Since they are owned by no one, there is no incentive to conserve them. If I don't catch the fish then someone else will – if I decide not to fish then it will make no difference to fish stocks. So I might as well fish. The proposed solution is to establish secure private property rights in all resources – including endangered species – which will provide private owners with the incentives to conserve resources and use them at the "optimal" rate. Furthermore, it is argued, markets will solve the problem of running out of particular resources since their scarcity will cause their prices to rise and induce the development of new products, synthetic rubber replacing natural rubber being but one example. Market signals, in the form of prices, therefore act to deter consumption of scarce resources and provide the incentive for innovation to find alternative sources or substitute resources. Establishing functioning markets for natural resources, such as water, is the key to their conservation.

Whether introducing more capitalism will save the rainforests, which cover 2 per cent of the Earth's surface but contain 40–50 per cent of all life forms, and which are currently being destroyed at the rate of over 30 million hectares per year (an area larger than Poland), is open to doubt.[10] Certainly, the historical precedent of the bison, whose numbers in North America were reduced from 60 million in 1800 to less than 60,000 by 1890 as capitalism swept the continent, is not encouraging.[11]

To conclude this chapter, let us recap the arguments of the proponents of capitalism. Capitalism is a natural economic system in that it is based on the institution of the market, an institution which comes "naturally" to humans and which arises "spontaneously" in all human societies. The market enables us to express our humanity (Smith) and provides us with a source of freedom (the Friedmans). To restrict the operations of the market therefore constitutes oppression. The profit motive provides capitalism with the incentives for dynamism, a dynamism which allows (competitive) capitalism to allocate resources efficiently in the short run and to maximize growth in the long run. Both the market and the profit motive require the institution of private property for their successful operation, an institution which can be justified morally and pragmatically. Indeed, the pragmatic argument for capitalism – it works better than other economic forms of organization – is widely held. The essential elements of the case for capitalism, as summarized, have remained basically unchanged since Smith was writing in the eighteenth century.

In addition to these properties, capitalism is also associated with political democracy, although whether this association is the result of a causal relationship is open to dispute. Capitalism, it is argued, makes for a just society in that it provides the basis for non-discrimination and provides protection for "minorities" through the "blindness" of the market. One of the functions of the minimal state is to uphold private property rights and to enforce voluntary contracts; another is to alleviate poverty, although the more conservative supporters of capitalism regard income redistribution as both morally and practically misguided. By providing incentives for minimizing the use of natural resources, and by markets sending price signals of scarcity, environmental objectives are best met with a capitalist system.

One of the characteristics of any analysis of capitalism is that it generates passion. That passion is evident in the normative assessments made of capitalism by its supporters. It is also evident in the assessments of its critics, and there are a host of reasons why capitalism can be seen as anything but "natural" and "free", as Chapter 3 will explain.

Further reading

For an examination of the different types of democracy, see Adam Przeworski's *Sustainable Democracy*, Cambridge: Cambridge University Press, 1995. The debate on the relationship between capitalism and democracy has received widespread attention. A classic in the field is Barrinton Moore's *Social Origins of Dictatorship and Democracy: Lord and Peasant in the Making of the Modern World*, Boston: Beacon Press, 1993. This book argues that there is no universal trend towards democracy. Instead, the paths towards democracy, fascism and communism are dependent upon historical conditions. See also Dietrich Rueschemeyer, Evelyne Huber Stephens and John Stephens, *Capitalist Development and Democracy*, Chicago: Chicago University Press, 1992. The implications of globalization for democracy are explored in Ronaldo Munck and Barry Gills (editors), *Globalization and Democracy*, The Annals of the American Academy of Political and Social Science, volume 581, 2002. For the debate on capitalism and democracy in developing countries see, for example, Paul Cammack, *Capitalism and Democracy in the Third World*, London: Leicester University Press, 1997. For the specifics of southeast Asia, see Garry Rodan, Kevin Hewison and Richard Robison (editors), *The Political Economy of Southeast Asia: Conflict, Crises and Change*, London: Oxford University Press, 2001. For data on the rise of democracy over the past 200 years, see the Polity IV Project at their website (http://www.cidcm.umd.edu/inscr/polity).

The case for market approaches to environmental problems is set out in Richard Sandor, Eric Bettelheim and Ian Swingland, "An overview of a free-market approach to climate change and conservation", in Ian Swingland (editor), *Capturing Carbon and Conserving Biodiversity: The Market Approach*, London: Earthscan, 2003.

Notes

1　As quoted in Greg Sheridan and Steve Lewis, "Free trade against terror", *The Australian*, 15 November 2002, p. 1.

2　This argument is made by Hall (1988).

3　It should be remembered that the "opium wars" of the 1840s were fought by Britain to ensure that British traders had the right to sell opium to the Chinese. To ensure that such rights were enforced, Britain took administrative control of Hong Kong for 150 years.

4　It is for this reason that authors such as Friedman haves argued that hybrid economic systems such as "market socialism" (in which markets operate fully but property is owned collectively) are not viable economic systems in the long run. See Friedman (1990).

5　On this point, see also Jameson (1991: 266).

6　McMillan's implied criteria for success in capitalism contrasts sharply, therefore, with Michael Moore's (2002: 44) description of George W. Bush's life: "Money and name alone have opened every door for you. Without effort or hard work or intelligence or ingenuity, you have been bequeathed a life of privilege."

7   We will review other interpretations of the East Asian style of capitalism in Chapter 5.

8   See Ferguson (2001: 9) for details.

9   Proportional taxation means that each person pays the same proportion of their income in tax. Progressive taxation occurs when higher-income groups pay a higher percentage of their income in tax than other income groups. Regressive taxation occurs when the poor pay a higher percentage of their income in tax than other income groups.

10   All figures from Rainforest Action Network (2003).

11   Figures from Adelaide Zoo.

CHAPTER 3

Capitalism as a system: "unjust" and "unstable"

Introduction

FOR CRITICS, CAPITALISM, far from representing the "triumph *of* the individual" as the pro-capitalist writers surveyed in the previous chapter argue, represents "triumph *over* the individual". According to a whole range of critics, capitalism subverts the individual's needs and aspirations to the demands of an economic system which is controlled by, and works in the interests of, a few. It is individuals – and the natural environment – which continually adjust to the demands of a profit-driven system and not the other way round. Capitalism does not "free" individuals but constrains the majority to work according to the dictates of a system over which it has no control.

For some critics this means that capitalism, as an economic system, must be reformed, managed or controlled to keep its destructive powers in check. The range of the market, the inviolable right to private property and the profit motive must all be harnessed, and sometimes restrained, by conscious intervention to promote the social good. For other, more radical, critics, it means that capitalism must be replaced by a different type of economic system, one which is not premised on the dominance of the market, private property and the profit motive.

To reformist and radical critics alike the capitalist system is unjust and unstable. To this, recent critics have added the charge that it is unsustainable, not just socially because of the inequality which it generates, but also environmentally.

Unjust and unstable: Keynes and reformist critics

Reformist critics argue that capitalism needs extensive regulation in the areas of both distribution and production. In terms of distribution, the outcomes of capitalism are seen as inequitable and as requiring a massive redistribution of resources within and between countries in order to achieve just social outcomes. In terms of production, the problem with capitalism is perceived as one of instability, causing large changes in economic conditions for the majority of the population. Policies fashioned after the views of John Maynard Keynes to stabilize the inherent volatility of capitalist production are typically seen as a solution to this.

As an example of the inequalities found in contemporary capitalism, consider the indicators presented by reformist critic Stephen Haseler (2000: xi): "some estimates calculate that the world's three richest people possess 'assets worth more than the combined gross domestic product of all of the least-developed countries', and others point out that the wealthiest 500 people own as much wealth as half of the population of the globe, and

500 hundred [*sic*] or so transnational corporations account for 80 per cent of world trade (and over 70 per cent of investment)."

These gross, even obscene, inequalities lead Haseler to describe the world we are living in as one of "super-rich capitalism" although it is, of course, super-rich only for the very few. What is more, Haseler's analysis of who is rich leads him to conclude (2000: xii) that "in today's global capitalism, rewards often tend to be higher for doing nothing, or next to nothing – accruing and using capital through inheritances – than for the hard work of securing skills in order to work for a living".

This observation is not, however, one that has just arisen "in today's global capitalism". Indeed, since industrial capitalism arose in the eighteenth and nineteenth centuries, socialists have been pointing to the scale of capitalist inequality. For example, socialist reformers of the mid-nineteenth century, including well-respected economists such as John Stuart Mill, all viewed the central problem of capitalism as the inverse relationship between work and rewards. These critics observed that those who did the hardest work received the least reward, while those who did not labour lived in affluence. Work and rewards in capitalist societies were inversely related![1] The solutions proposed by socialists such as John Stuart Mill were inheritance taxes designed to eliminate family wealth and high taxes on non-labour (or "unearned") income. These policies were adopted to various degrees by social democratic governments throughout Western Europe in the last half of the twentieth century. While the agenda for many governments now is for tax cuts to restore "incentives" and "fairness" to the tax system, it was not always thus.

Some of the capitalist–philanthropist–visionaries of the nineteenth century, such as Robert Owen with his New Lanark mills and Titus Salt with his Yorkshire mills, believed that workers would respond to better conditions by improving themselves. They provided their own prescriptions for an alternative society which departed from the Dickensian conditions then prevalent in industrializing Britain and now often repeated in industrializing Asia and elsewhere. Today, capitalist–philanthropist–visionary Anita Roddick's The Body Shop practised good corporate ethics and supported fair trade. But the problem of massive inequality in the rewards under capitalism remains, taxation and alternative business practices notwithstanding.

In terms of instability, capitalism has historically seen periods of growth and recession and, occasionally, depression. Periods of recession and depression have typically been blamed by the supporters of capitalism on the misguided actions of either the government or associations such as trade unions which have prevented labour markets from being sufficiently "flexible". As we saw in the previous chapter, capitalism is seen by its adherents as being self-regulating and free markets as being self-equilibrating.

Keynes, writing in the 1930s, challenged the underlying proposition of most economists of the time that the capitalist system was inherently stable and that price and wage flexibility would ensure that any disequilibria were temporary and self-correcting (Box 3.1).

The capitalist system was inherently unstable, according to Keynes. Workers' wage demands did not fluctuate greatly, yet the volume of employment did; the reason for unemployment could not therefore be that workers were demanding too much and that wages needed to be reduced, as orthodox theory in the 1930s required. For Keynes, the source of instability had to be

BOX 3.1

John Maynard Keynes: 1883–1946

Keynes was one of the most influential figures of the twentieth century. Born into privilege, he went from Eton to King's College, Cambridge and on to the British Civil Service where he served in the India Office. He went back to Cambridge as an academic but returned to the civil service with the Treasury during the First World War. Keynes attended the Versailles Peace Conference in 1918 but later resigned in protest at the unfairness of the reparations payments imposed upon Germany. A prolific author, Keynes soon afterwards published *The Economic Consequences of the Peace* in which he criticized the post-First World War settlement. His most famous book, *The General Theory of Employment, Interest and Money*, was published in 1936. Coming at a time when much of the world was suffering from the grip of the Great Depression, the book criticized prevailing policies aimed at reducing wages as the way of increasing employment levels. Keynes's ideas transformed economic thinking throughout much of the world and a whole branch of economics, Keynesian economics, was developed in the post-1945 period. Keynes himself led the British delegation to the Bretton Woods conference in 1944 which sought to provide a stable framework for post-1945 growth, a framework which included setting up the IMF and the World Bank.

Not only an economist, Keynes was also a member of the literary "Bloomsbury Group" and a chairman of the British Arts Council.

found elsewhere. He identified the volatility of investment as the key cause of instability under capitalism. This instability arose because investment decisions were based on entrepreneurs' "animal spirits" (1973: 161). As such, these spirits were presumably "natural" but their result was that capitalism was based on spirits which inevitably produced instability. Investment decisions by firms were based on expectations of the future, expectations which were premised on what Keynes (1973: 148) termed "the state of confidence". Business confidence could easily be affected by political events on the other side of the world. And if business confidence fell then investment would be postponed or scrapped and, as a result, the demand for labour would fall and unemployment would rise. The unconstrained workings of the capitalist economy would therefore produce continual swings in the level of employment matching the swings in entrepreneurs' confidence about the future and reflected in their investment spending.

An interventionist state capable of counteracting the volatilities of private investment decisions and stabilizing the economy to ensure full employment was needed in Keynes's view. It was the task of government, therefore, to adjust its own spending levels and use the instruments at its disposal – such as monetary and fiscal policy – to stabilize the capitalist economy in the face of fluctuating private investment levels. Many governments in the advanced capitalist countries accepted this as their role, even duty, for three decades after 1945. Capitalism was the preferred economic system, but it was one which needed to be managed by an interventionist state in order to minimize the costs that it otherwise inevitably imposed upon society, most notably in the form of unemployment.

New forms of instability have emerged and "casino capitalism" is what we have today.[2] Or so its critics say, referring to the gambling mentality that leads to wild swings in the values of stock markets and currencies. In the wake of these wild swings, the lives of workers and ordinary people are disrupted

BOX 3.2

The Tobin Tax

A tax on international currency transactions designed to prevent speculative capital flows. Named after its proponent, Nobel Prize-winning economist James Tobin, the idea is that the tax would be set high enough to deter speculators from moving "hot money" around the world at short notice and would therefore reduce the threat of the type of currency crises that engulfed Asia in 1997, Brazil in 1998 and Argentina in 2001. The tax would be low enough that longer-term investment flows would not be deterred. A taxation rate in the order of 0.25 per cent (that is, 25 cents per $100) is typically suggested. Some economists are sceptical whether this would be high enough to deter speculation. Many in power argue that the tax wouldn't work unless all countries agreed to introduce it; and since all won't agree, the tax is not feasible. Nevertheless, many social activists have taken up the cause, arguing that it would prevent destabilization arising from international capital flows and provide anywhere from $100 billion to $300 billion a year in tax revenue which could be used to reduce world poverty and to address world environmental problems.

and damaged, as the Asian crisis in 1997 demonstrated. To prevent the destabilizing excesses of international financial markets, various proposals have been made to tame the markets. The most famous of these is the "Tobin tax" (Box 3.2).

These critiques of the inequality and instability arising from capitalism have pointed to the need for strong state interventions in the "free market" to correct these outcomes. A more radical conclusion – that of replacing capitalism with an alternative form of economic organization – has been advanced by those influenced by the Marxist analysis of capitalism.

Unjust and unstable: Marx and radical critics

For Karl Marx (Box 3.3), the logic of capitalism as a system, premised on the need to generate private profits, produced a system that was both dynamic and capable of enormous productivity but one which was also rooted in class antagonism, inequality, inhumanity and crises. It was a system which represented a specific historic phase (and therefore not a timeless "natural" system) and one which would not last forever (as "the end of history").

BOX 3.3

Karl Marx (1818–1883) and
Friedrich Engels (1820–1895)

Authors of *The Communist Manifesto* in 1848, Marx and Engels exhorted the workers of the world to unite. Why? Because they had nothing to lose but their chains: the chains of "wage slavery" under which they sold their labour "freely" but still ended up chained to a system over which they had no control and which did not serve their interests. The underlying theoretical analysis of this and the political struggles resulting from it filled their life's work. Marx, a journalist as well as a scholarly writer, was born in Trier, Germany but moved between Bonn, Paris and Brussels before settling in London in 1849. Working in poverty for much of his life, he wrote prolifically. His major analysis of the economic workings of the capitalist system, *Das Kapital* [*Capital*], appeared in three volumes, although only one of them, Volume 1 published in 1867, did so in his lifetime. His friend, collaborator and financial supporter, Friedrich Engels, published the two final volumes after Marx's death.

Engels, the son of a Lancashire textile manufacturer, worked with Marx to develop the theory of "historical materialism". This theory argued that it was the economic base of society which determined its political, social and ideological character. Ideas did not exist independently but were a function of the economic organization of society. Capitalism produced its own social character and its own ideology, "bourgeois ideology". This ideology typically portrayed the interests of capitalists as everyone's interests or as the "national interest". It also promoted as "freedom" the workings of an oppressive system. Engels also published much on his own, including the important *The Condition of the Working Class in England* in 1845 which still stands as an important essay in social history. His *Origins of the Family, Private Property and the State* (1884) is an important work on gender relations under capitalism.

Marx and Engels were only marginally influential in their own time, but as socialist and communist revolutions swept much of the world in the twentieth century, at one time around one-third of the world's population was living in states which called themselves "Marxist". Few of these states were actually faithful to many of Marx's ideas.

Workers entered the labour market with nothing to sell but their "hides" and, as a result, received "a hiding" (Marx 1954: 176). Marx argued that capitalism was based on exactly this – the exploitation of the working class by the capitalist class. Although it might appear that the buyers and sellers of labour met "equally" in the marketplace and entered "freely" into con-tracts with each other for mutual gain, this masked the reality of the capitalist system. The capitalists had a monopoly of the means of production (firms) while workers had only their capa-city to work to sell. This was the basis of capitalist production: capitalists who owned firms hired workers who owned only their own labour, and the former sought to use the labour that they hired to make a profit for themselves.

Capitalist production was characterized by a central antagonism: the interests of workers and capitalists were diametrically opposed. It was in the interests of the workers to work as little as possible for as much reward as possible, and it was in the interests of the capitalists to extract as much effort as possible from workers while paying them as little as possible.

It is for this reason that workplaces contain a variety of "monitoring devices" from clocking-in machines, line managers and supervisors, time and motion studies, to the whole battery of techniques taught in MBA programmes, which are necessary to ensure that the worker works for as long as, and as intensely as, the capitalist owners of the firm can enforce. Sweatshops around the world, often associated with the garment industry from China to New York, offer classic examples of this without having to recall the factory system of the nineteenth century described by Marx and Dickens. But the basic dynamics are applicable to all other capitalist industries from manufacturing to services. The interests of employers are to have employees work as intensely as possible and to have as few restrictions on "management prerogatives" as possible. The employees, meanwhile, have interests in resisting the control of their lives by their employers.

To advance their interests, employers not only rely on the "sticks" described as "monitoring devices" above, but may also rely on a "divide and conquer" strategy, with many grades in the workforce which encourage workers to pursue individual career advancement (rather than common causes), as well as on "carrots" such as incentive pay and productivity bonuses. Workers are brought together to perform economic functions in capitalist firms, but employers devise methods designed to prevent them from acting together politically as a class. Such a system inevitably produces tensions and conflict within the firm and within the wider political arena. As I will show in Chapter 5, one of the major ways in which capitalist societies differ is precisely in the ways in which they have sought to manage these conflicts between capital and labour.

Capitalism is a structure of "unfreedom". Workers are not, as in the Friedman analysis, "free to choose" but are destined only to fill roles as wage earners; workers, having only their capacity to labour to sell, have no choice but to sell it. The capitalist system does not work for their benefit but workers are incorporated into it as essential, yet expendable, elements. The individual does not matter in the capitalist system; he or she can be hired and fired as necessary. The individual's concerns, material or otherwise, are of interest to the capitalist only to the extent that they impinge upon the employee's capacity to labour. All that matters is that workers, as a class, are available to meet the requirements of profit-seeking production when, if, and how required. The worker, under capitalism, is needed to sell his or her capacity to labour.

The importance of labour – or why workers are alienated but apes aren't

Workers are robbed of their humanity by being forced to sell their capacity to labour. The defining characteristic of humans was not, as Smith had argued, their "propensity to truck, barter and exchange" but their capacity to labour. Responding to the Darwinian agenda, Engels (1962) argued, in an essay entitled "The part played by labour in the transition from ape to man", that the evolutionary jump occurred with the ability to labour.

The conditions under which we labour therefore define our humanity. In the capitalist system, it is precisely the control over our labour which is given up when entering into wage contracts with the capitalist. The capacity to labour now becomes the property of the capitalist – the product of the worker's labour owned by another. Workers are "alienated" from the product of their own labour. For workers, the capitalist system is both alienating – losing control of their labour and the root of their humanity – and exploiting, serving the interests of the capitalist class rather than their own (Box 3.4).

BOX 3.4

Forms of alienation under capitalism

The theme of alienation under capitalism, and the ways in which capitalism robs us of our humanity, is a recurrent one. For example, Australian political economist Frank Stilwell (2000) argues that four types of alienation can be identified in contemporary capitalist societies. The first he terms "economic alienation" and this refers to the alienation of the employee in the workplace as discussed by Marx but still relevant today. Despite the increases in wages and material possessions which have accrued to workers in many capitalist countries, we appear to be no happier in submitting to capitalist imperatives in controlling our work. Contemporary capitalism encourages us to find happiness as consumers, but at work alienation continues and we should expect no more than to be subjected to the demands of the bottom-line. And compliance with these demands is being increasingly enforced. For example, economist David Gordon (1996) documented how US corporations in the 1980s and 1990s, far from becoming "lean and mean", became "fat and mean" as the ratio of managers and supervisors to production workers rose in order to exert more control over how work was performed.

The ability of employees to control their labour, or to exercise democracy in the workplace, is strictly limited in capitalist firms.

To this economic alienation, Stilwell (2000: 93) adds three other types: (i) environmental alienation, as evidenced by the subjugation of Nature to the requirements of production, with the result that we feel alienated from our natural environment; (ii) social alienation, as evidenced by the process of marginalization or social exclusion in which a significant part of the expendable working class becomes further and further removed from the mainstream of society; and (iii) political alienation, as evidenced by growing apathy among voters and cynicism towards political processes which seem not to reflect individuals' interests or concerns and where the voices of the majorities seem to be seldom heard. There is a "democratic deficit". Certainly, with the TV audience for the 2000 Superbowl exceeding the voter turnout in the Presidential election of that year, political alienation has reached high proportions in the US, the world's leading capitalist country.

Capitalism's message to its workers, as emblazoned on placards at anti-globalization protests, is to "work, consume, be silent, die". Faced with this message, and being alienated from their labour, many seek meaning and identity through other activities such as religion (the "opium of the masses" in Marx's phrase), consumerism, drugs or sport. The pursuit of personal freedom and human solidarity is denied by capitalist control of the economic organization of society and so has to be found outside the production arena. Even the new masters of the information age, the computer whizz-kids, are not immune. As Aune (2001: 163) writes: "if personal computing and the Internet promise individual empowerment, more meaningful work, and greater democracy, these promises are unlikely to be fulfilled fully under capitalism as we know it".

What is needed, therefore, is a radical change in the economic organization of society so that human liberation is a possibility. The choice that Marx presented us with is between capitalist barbarism and socialist civilization. This choice is presented to us today as the choice between global capitalism and democracy.[3] Global capitalism, promoted as the handmaiden of representative democracy by its supporters, is seen as the nemesis of substantive democracy by its critics.

Capitalism's contradiction: poverty amidst plenty

At the same time that capitalism alienates the individual, the material benefits which it brings are not available to all. This goes beyond simply the income and wealth inequalities highlighted by reformist critics. It also appears, Marx pointed out, as a central contradiction of capitalism in that it permits the existence of excess capacity at the same time as there are unmet social needs. Capitalism is simply unable to put resources to their full use, even where demonstrable needs exist, because resources are deployed for the pursuit of private profit and not for the satisfaction of social needs. As a result, unemployed construction workers coexist with homeless people. Some parts of the world produce huge food surpluses and farms go bankrupt while hundreds of millions in other parts of the world are chronically undernourished; according to the United Nations 30 per cent of all children under the age of five in sub-Saharan Africa are underweight, 48 per cent in South-Central Asia and 19 per cent in Western Asia.[4] Furthermore, in the US, the richest country that the world has ever seen, 41 per cent of children below the age of six grow up living in or near poverty.[5] Capitalism is unable to address these contradictions; its inner logic of profit-making makes the logic of using resources to meet social needs unworkable.

According to one analyst of capitalism, "when it comes to catering to the wants and desires of every individual, no matter how trivial those wants seem to others, no system does it even half so well" (Thurow 1996: 1). This assessment tells only half the story. It is true that in responding to consumers' material wants, wherever they come from, for the majority of the population in most countries the capitalist system performs this function reasonably well, and particularly well for wealthy individuals with trivial desires. However, it fails miserably to fill the needs of those who have no demand because they have no income. The rise of homelessness on the streets of every Western city in the past 30 years and the permanence of food banks demonstrate that capitalism is failing to meet many people's daily wants even in relatively rich societies. At the global level, UNICEF reports that "more than 10 million children die each year, although most of those deaths could be prevented" (2002, para. 48). Entirely non-trivial wants and desires are not being met by a capitalist world system which cannot match production for profit with distribution for needs.

The latest example of this contradiction is found with the HIV/AIDS pandemic. The UN estimates that this affects 42 million people worldwide, the vast majority of whom go untreated because they cannot afford the necessary expensive drugs produced by large pharmaceutical companies and cheaper "generic" varieties would violate patent protection. The AIDS example provides a dramatic example of the contradiction of capitalism. On one side are the private property patent rights of multinational corporations in the world's most profitable industry. On the other side are literally the lives of millions of the world's poor, mostly in sub-Saharan Africa.[6] However, the two sides cannot, under the logic of capitalism, meet because as Dr Harvey Bale Jr, of the International Federation of Pharmaceutical Manufacturers' Associations, stated, "there is no marketplace to speak of in the poor world".[7] And if there are no profits to be made, the needs of millions go unmet.

The AIDS example simply provides further evidence of how the logic of capitalism operates: if you have money, capitalism is likely to provide you with many material choices, including some of the most trivial ones; if you lack money, then free-market capitalism will leave you without any choices at all even for your most basic needs, including life itself.

According to analyses based on the work of Marx, therefore, capitalism is unjust in that it leads to distributional outcomes which do not take account of social need but which are bound by the logic of profit-making. The vast majority of individuals, who make up the ranks of the wage-earners, are denied their humanity by a system which separates them from their work and also leads to political, social and environmental alienation. The system is also regarded as unstable.

Capitalism and crises

Capitalism is seen as crisis-ridden and leading towards monopoly. Crisis here means a crisis for the capitalist class; and this occurs when profits fall to levels unacceptable to capitalists. One cause of crisis can be seen in the workings of the business cycle. In the boom period of the cycle, profit expectations are high and investment is high. The demand for labour is high and as a result unemployment falls and wages start to be bid up. However, after a while, the rise in wages eats into capitalist profits and creates a "crisis", that is a crisis of profitability. This is "solved" by capitalists reducing their investment levels, with the result that growth falls and unemployment increases until workers are disciplined to accept lower wages; at this point profit expectations pick up and the whole cycle is repeated. Unemployment therefore plays an important role in the capitalist economy by weakening the bargaining power of labour; it is not an accidental or unfortunate by-product but an inevitable feature of capitalism. Another important part of the process involved in the business cycle as outlined above is that, in the crisis period, firm restructuring takes place in order to create the conditions for renewed profitability. This restructuring takes the form of mergers and acquisitions with the result that monopolies, far from being an aberration caused by government policy as Friedman asserts, are another integral and inevitable feature of capitalism.

Capitalism as anti-Nature

Recent critics of capitalism have added to the list of its inadequacies environmental destruction and ecological unsustainability.[8] There are two arguments which are relevant here.

The first argument views capitalism as a mode of thinking based upon the eighteenth-century Enlightenment tradition of human mastery over Nature. It is a system premised on the desirability of industrialization with its emphasis on a human-centred, rather than an ecology-centred, view of the world. It is a system which focuses on the use of resources in pursuit of economic growth, assuming that these resources are limitless. On this reading, capitalism is one of the most prominent systems of economic organization, but only one of many (state socialism being another) which promote the non-sustainable use of the Earth's resources.

A second strand of ecologist thinking, associated with eco-socialists, argues that capitalism has specific characteristics that make it inimical to environmental sustainability (rather than being just one among several economic systems that equally share this trait). According to this view, it is the driving force of profits and the need to expand, together with capitalism's maldistribution of world income, that produce widespread poverty in developing countries, which is to blame for environmental destruction. Monoculture farming practices, genetically modified foods, the destruction of virgin habitats, pollution, and poverty-induced land degradation can all be laid at the door of capitalism's insatiable desire for profits. Capitalism, proclaimed as "natural" by its proponents, is in fact "anti-Nature".

For environmentalists, the task is to stop viewing Nature as a resource to be used in the pursuit of profit but to rethink Nature as a "trust". Expressed in different terms, the task is to "de-commodify" Nature. The concept of a "commodity" is central to Marx's analysis of capitalism. A commodity is simply any product that is produced for sale on the market. Under capitalism labour becomes a commodity, something that is sold on the market. And this is true for a wide range of products; capitalism is therefore a process of "commodification", of producing goods (and images) for sale on the market driven by the profit motive. More recently, this process of commodification has driven capitalism to explore new forms of commodities with the ownership of life itself, in the form of genes and biotechnology, now on the agenda. Natural resources such as water are now entering commodity production. Capitalism is therefore seen as a relentless process of commodification, leading to the marketization of ever more aspects of human existence as the search for profits, the driving force of capitalism, must be satisfied in new ways. Nature has not been exempt from this process; Nature, although not produced for the market, nevertheless becomes treated under capitalism *as if* it were a commodity, as something to be owned privately and used profitably. It is a specific feature of capitalist societies to treat Nature as a commodity, a feature which is not found in other societies such as many indigenous societies, for example. For many of the latter, Nature has always been a "trust".

To conclude the review of the critics of capitalism, I will examine two issues considered in the last chapter where the implications of capitalism for social equality and the characteristics of the political system were analysed. The first issue questions why, if capitalism is blind and treats everyone equally, there are significant gender inequalities in capitalist societies. The second issue is how reformist and radical critics view the role of the state.

Capitalism and gender inequality

Women in capitalist societies typically do more household labour, are more likely to be living in poverty, are more likely to be in low-paying jobs, have less wealth and are under-represented in positions of power. In many countries, they face discrimination in the labour market as well as various degrees of abuse, including sexual abuse, in the workplace and in the household. Why should this be the case? Is this because of something inherent in the workings of capitalism?

These questions have attracted considerable attention from feminist scholars. While there has been no consensus on the relationship between patriarchy (a system of male dominance) and the specific features of capitalism, a few central questions and propositions will be outlined here.

The view that women's subordinate position in society can be attributed to capitalism can be traced back to Engels. He argued, in his essay on *The Origins of Private Property, the State, and the Family* (1972), that the onset of capitalism destroyed a pre-capitalist period of sexual equality and resulted in the "domestic slavery" of the wife. The argument he made was that in pre-capitalist societies, there was a division of labour based on sex in which the female was primarily responsible for child rearing and for the running of the household, much of which was performed communally, while the male took primary responsibility for food procurement and trading. However, although each partner had "separate spheres", they were "equal" since the activities which were performed by each partner were equally valued in terms of their usefulness for household survival. With the onset of capitalism, however, private property arose and this was appropriated by men who had primary responsibility for market-based activity. With this appropriation of private property and the private accumulation of wealth by men, they were placed in a dominant position within the household and within society, with "women's work" in the home now being less valued. In short, the capitalist system is a gendered system which neither recognizes nor counts women's work. Subsequent feminist analysis has documented and analysed how women have historically been denied access to private property and have been excluded from market activities; women have a quite different relationship to capitalism than men as a result.

According to this analysis, patriarchy arose from the central features of capitalism. For others, however, the experience of women's oppression in non-capitalist societies, including the former socialist countries, has demonstrated that patriarchy and capitalism are separate processes. Indeed, capitalism can be seen as a system which has historically broken down some of the forces of patriarchy.[9] Capitalism has increasingly brought women into the labour force and given them some forms of economic independence through wage-earning possibilities. In this sense, capitalism can be seen as progressive in that it has increased women's economic independence and, if earning income in the market is related to power relations within the household, then it has reduced gender inequality.

That said, however, it is also clear that capitalism assigns to women particular roles both inside and outside the paid labour market. Women still perform the major portion of household labour regardless of their participation in the paid labour market and are still found segregated in the workplace in predominantly low-paid positions and occupations. This is as true, for example, for secretarial work, child-care centres, and the nursing profession in Western countries as it is for electronics assembly workers in Asia. While all of these jobs are "skilful", the social construction of "skill" has meant that these are jobs in which skill is not well rewarded, whereas the skills found in more traditional male employments (such as road construction, engineering and medical surgery) are better rewarded.

Part of the complexity in explaining women's subordinate position derives not simply from establishing the relationships between patriarchy and capitalism, but also because the role of women in capitalist economies has changed over time. In Western countries, women's traditional role in raising the family and taking care of the household led to the ideology of the "male breadwinner". Women's contributions to the household as "unpaid domestic labour" were theorized as important for capitalism since they provided the next generation of workers but without being paid directly for it. Women were brought into the workforce either to fill gaps left by men in areas such as cleaning and nursing or in times of national emergency such as in munitions factories in wartime. But this was still uncommon and women in Western societies were primarily home-makers.

From the 1970s onwards, however, when multinational firms began more systematically moving production to developing countries in order to take advantage of lower labour costs, they displayed a preference for employing the so-called "nimble fingers" of the unorganized pool of young, unmarried (or, more accurately, pre-married) female workers.[10] Furthermore, in the West, real wages have been stagnant for close to three decades and the only way that household incomes have been able to increase is by women increasingly entering the labour force. Women now have significantly higher labour market participation rates than in the pre-1970 period and there has been what some commentators have referred to as the "feminization" of the global labour force.[11] No longer excluded from the capitalist labour market, women are now very much part of it. It is only in the former Soviet bloc, where the destruction and restructuring of industry in those countries' transition to capitalism has been occurring, that women's presence in the labour force is being significantly reduced.

As this transformation has occurred, and as women have increasingly entered the paid labour market, capitalism is faced with a problem in how to "care" for its societies' members. Leading feminist scholar Nancy Folbre (2001) has argued that in the past caring was performed in capitalist (and other) economies by women who were assigned the "duty" of caring by patriarchal rules and norms which defined what was "women's work". However, as contemporary capitalism has drawn more and more women into the labour force, capitalism now confronts a crisis of caring. She raises the questions "Is it possible for capitalist societies to be caring societies?" and "Who will do the caring, and on what basis?"

Part of the answer is to be found in the emergence of a "global caring chain" according to feminist sociologist Arlie Russell Hochschild (2000). She argues that the market for one type of care, mothering, in the US used to be predominantly nationally based, typically on class and race lines, with black women in the South, Mexican–American women in the Southwest and Asian–American women in the West, caring for middle-class white children. Now, the pattern has become increasingly global-ized with women from the Philippines or Jamaica, for example, migrating to the US to work as nannies in order to send remit-tances back to their families and children in their home country. The "caring chain" has become global; as Hochschild notes (2000: 131), "one of the common forms of such a chain is: (1) an older daughter from a poor family who cares for her siblings while (2) her mother works as a nanny caring for the children of a migrating nanny who, in turn, (3) cares for the child of a family in a rich country". In this way, care is being globalized, with middle-class kids in advanced countries receiving the care and attention of Third World nannies who have left their own children behind. Are we witnessing, Hochschild (2000: 135) asks us, a situation where "First world countries such as the United States [are] importing maternal love as they have imported copper, zinc, gold and other ores from Third World countries in the past"?

The emergence of global care chains points to the dynamism of the system and how it attempts to "solve" the need for caring. Even here, though, left unresolved is who cares for poorer members of societies? Capitalism is unable to provide a solution to this problem, with the result that, especially in their most free-market incarnations, capitalist societies are witnessing increasing social malaise. Responses have included unenlightened attempts to recapture the past by pushing women back into the home "where they belong". Only single mothers living on social security or welfare are exempt as they are increasingly told that they do not belong in the home but must stop caring for their young children and obtain work. More enlightened responses, such as extending parental and maternal paid leaves, have been adopted in some countries. However, the central question remains: how will capitalist societies organize for the care of their members? And what will the implications be for women? It is these types of questions which cause so much difficulty for the proponents of capitalism whose lens is entirely that of the market. While they view the market as a site of "economic freedom", they fail to locate "the market" within the wider context of human activity which includes non-market activity. This is important for women because they have been seen as being primarily responsible for much of the non-market activity, a responsibility which necessarily affects how they participate in the market sphere. It is important for us all as we all have interests in ensuring that society is caring.

The capitalist state: to be captured or replaced?

The discussion of gender inequality under capitalism raises interesting questions concerning the role of the state. Is it an institution which can be "captured" to advance the interests of women? For many writers the answer is clearly "yes". Laws and policies such as those on non-discrimination, equal pay and maternity benefits, for example, all represent ways in which the state can be used to protect and advance the interests of women.

The same can be said of workers who can gain through industrial relations legislation, the regulation of working hours, workplace safety and conditions and unemployment benefits, for example. More generally, the institutional apparatus of the state has been seen by a wide variety of authors and political parties as a means to manage capitalism, maintaining its essential economic dynamism but modifying and ameliorating its negative social outcomes. Keynesian macroeconomic policy was discussed above as a way of controlling the instability of capitalism. The welfare state, with its array of economic supports, is aimed at overcoming the economic insecurity experienced by workers and vulnerable groups. In an important way, the welfare state weakens the link between labour market participation and standard of living with the result that labour is, at least partly, "de-commodified". The taxation system can be used as a powerful instrument of income redistribution, while state provision of education can enhance social mobility and provide equality of opportunity.

These policies have been central to a range of social democratic and left parties in the post-war period and are claimed as the intellectual heritage of those, such as Blair, pursuing the so-called "Third Way". Social democratic governments in Scandinavia have gone further and pursued policies which have attempted to permanently institutionalize labour's involvement in the running of the economy and have required capitalists to act in accordance with wider social objectives, including full employment. The ways in which capital–labour relations have been mediated by the state is a major theme of the historically focused Chapters 4, 5 and 6 of this book.

For reformist critics of capitalism, capturing the state offers the possibility of managing capitalism to produce more economically and socially desirable outcomes. For radical critics, however, the state under capitalism is not a vehicle which can bring long-term social transformation. Scepticism over the claims for the state's transformative role arises from an analysis of both its general and specific actions, actions which demonstrate the state's role in upholding capitalism.

In some countries, this may be all too clear. For example, in strife-torn West Papua, US-owned mining company Freeport Indonesia pays the Indonesian military to provide security for its gold and copper mining operations.[12] This provides a good example of how ruling elites in many developing countries use the power of the state to protect the interests of private capital. Radical sociologist James Petras (2002: 464) has made the same point with respect to Latin America when he refers to the "servile peon presidents of the continent serving the [interests of the US] empire". Furthermore, critics of capitalism also point out that there is no necessary reason for capitalism to lead to representative democracy; in many parts of the world, the interests of capitalists are well served by repressive states.

But what of democratic states? Can they be effectively captured? To analyse these questions, consider the state in Western Europe. In general terms, the origins of the modern European state can be traced back to the transformations which led to the rising capitalist class "capturing" the state from the landed aristocratic class and (in some cases) the monarchy. Michel Beaud (2001: 42) describes this process as follows: "when the bourgeoisie felt itself strong enough to dominate the world market, it abandoned mercantilist theses in favor of the virtues of free trade. When it felt strong enough to confront absolutism, it both armed itself with the new ideas of freedom and free consent (thereby gaining petty bourgeois and popular support) and allied itself with the enlightened layers of the nobility (which wanted to quiet rumblings of peasant uprisings and popular discontent)."

In the specific case of France, Beaud argues (2001: 67) that "the main aspirations of the bourgeoisie were attained in the revolution of 1789: the abolition of privileges, the dismantling of the corporative order of guild wardenships, the abolishment of the privileges of trading companies, and the suppression of mining company monopolies. The king was swept away in the great whirlwind of revolution." Within two years, however, laws were passed which labelled as "riots" any meetings by workers organized to discuss their common interests. As Beaud (2001: 67) continues, "its victory against the nobility appearing to be assured, the bourgeoisie was already protecting itself against the working classes".

Governments throughout the capitalist world enacted similar legislation designed to open up business to new entrants and to enhance profitability by suppressing workers' organizations. Could a state, fashioned in this way to support the interests of capitalists against other classes, be "captured" again by the long struggles for trade union recognition and for universal suffrage? If this is the case, then the explanation for the rise of democracy with capitalism is not to be found in the role played by the middle class, as capitalism's supporters often suggest. Rather, the struggles to extend the franchise were undertaken by ordinary men and women, the workers in the system, seeking to advance their interests. The battle for the principle of "one person, one vote" was a hard-fought one, based on the struggles and protests of workers' organizations and feminist groups. But is the democratic capitalist state capable of advancing the interests of the mass of the population? Is it capable of transforming itself into something else?

This question can be addressed at the practical level. Critics point to the private wealth needed to run for election, particularly in the US, where all attempts at reforming "campaign finance" seem to have very little effect and mainstream political life favours those of independent wealth and with generous corporate backers. But there is a more important theoretical level at which the question should also be addressed. At the general level, the modern state is seen as owing its primary allegiance to the survival of capitalism; there may be some scope for gains, even large gains in some historical periods, for ordinary citizens, but ultimately the state's function is to preserve capitalism. Particularly during times of crisis, therefore, the state can be expected to act in favour of capital and against labour in restructuring social relations and the organization of society in ways which permit capitalism – and the conditions for profit-making –

to survive. The state is not the impartial referee; it is the enforcer of capitalists' interests.

The capitalist state and education: enforcing the rules of American football or those of the treadmill?

The ambiguity of the capitalist state can be seen by examining the education system. The education system is typically regarded by reformist social democrats as well as by capitalism's proponents as a critical vehicle for social mobility and for minimizing the importance of class structures in determining personal advancement. Radical critics view it as playing a much less liberating role and as an important part in supporting the capitalist system. Consider, for example, the arguments of US radical critics Samuel Bowles and Herb Gintis. In their book, *Schooling in Capitalist America* (1976), they argued that the education system must be seen within the larger context of the "people production process" which "in the workplace and in schools . . . is dominated by the imperatives of profit and domination rather than human need. The unavoidable necessity of growing up and getting a job in the United States forces us all to become less than we could be: less free, less secure, in short less happy" (1976: 53–54). The education system contributes to this restriction on freedom by harnessing schools to produce the skills required by the capitalist labour market, by reinforcing fragmentation in the workforce by streaming and other status groups within the classroom, and by reinforcing the ideology that life's rewards are a function of individual efforts rather than class structures. As a result, they argue that the education system in the US has been relatively successful in meeting the goal of maintaining social stability but has not fared well in promoting personal development or social equity (Bowles and Gintis 1988: 235–236).

Their arguments are reinforced by the recent emphasis on education as a way of preparing everyone to "compete" in the global economy. The stress on the need for education and retraining has been pushed by governments of all political persuasions, and perhaps more strongly by centre-left parties, which have seen expanding education and (re)training programmes as key components of their interventionism. This strategy is based on the assumption that the primary reason for unemployment is the mismatch between workers' skills and the needs of the "new economy" rather than an overall lack of jobs. It also presupposes that all individuals and countries can successfully pursue the same policy. But at the country level, the whole point of the strategy is to attract mobile capital by the availability of highly skilled local labour. If other countries are playing the same game then success is far from guaranteed. The proliferation of call centres in countries like India, for example, where highly educated labour is available at a fraction of the cost of that in advanced countries, suggests that competition between states will inevitably lead to winners and losers.

The strategy of increasing education and skill levels for individuals and countries works only for as long as you are one step ahead of the competition (and have no concern for the well-being of those who are "less competitive"). The education example indicates that a more appropriate sporting analogy for global capitalism is not McMillan's American football (McMillan 2002) but the treadmill as suggested by David Coates. He argues (2000: 254), in an analogy as applicable to individuals as it is to nation states, that "you cannot get off the treadmill simply by running faster. All you can do by that mechanism is temporarily pass others, until they respond by running faster too, with the long-term consequence of having the whole field increase their speed just to stand still. The victor in such a race is not the runner, but the treadmill."

Just as individuals now need degrees to obtain jobs which were available to school leavers 20 years ago, so countries must provide ever more educated workforces to keep attracting the same amount of foreign investment; it is the employers and the multinationals who gain from this. And it is the capitalist states' education and retraining policies for a "competitive" world which are aiding them. Furthermore, it is the capitalist state's ultimate role as the guarantor of capitalism that leads to high levels of political alienation; governments cannot respond to the genuine needs and aspirations of their populations because they are constrained by supporting an economic system which prevents these needs and aspirations being met.

For radical critics, what is required is not a managed capitalism with the capitalist state smoothing capitalism's rough edges where possible but enforcing its logic when necessary. Rather, a radical social transformation is needed to bring about an alternative system of economic organization which empowers individuals and societies – an alternative based on individual liberty, collective solidarity and substantive democracy; an alternative to the subjugation of individuals and societies to the rapacious demands of capitalism. This is a quite different normative assessment of capitalism, as an abstract system, to that presented in Chapter 2.

In Chapters 4, 5 and 6, I will turn my focus to examining capitalism historically.

Further reading

The extent of global inequalities is neatly summarized in Bob Sutcliffe's *100 Ways of Seeing an Unequal World*, London: Zed Books, 2001. Also useful are reports by United Nations agencies such as UNICEF, UNDP and UNIFEM. Most of their publications are available on their websites.

For the life and thought of many reformers and radicals, including John Stuart Mill, John Maynard Keynes, Karl Marx and Friedrich Engels, see chapters in Robert Heilbroner's very readable *The Worldly Philosophers*, New York: Simon and Schuster, 2000.

The case for a Tobin-style tax is reviewed in Alex Michalos's *Good Taxes: The Case for Taxing Foreign Currency Exchange and Other Financial Transactions*, Toronto: University of Toronto Press, 1997. For a good review of the debates over capitalism and the environment, see Neil Carter, *The Politics of the Environment: Ideas, Activism and Policy*, Cambridge: Cambridge University Press, 2001. For an environmentalist position on Nature as a "trust" see, for example, Herman Daly and John Cobb, *For the Common Good: Redirecting the Economy Toward Community, the Environment and a Sustainable Future*, Boston: Beacon Press, 1994.

The impacts of capitalism on gender and race are discussed for the US in Teresa Amott and Julia Mattaei, *Race, Gender and Work: A Multicultural Economic History of Women in the United States*, South End Press, 1996. For Australia, see Rhonda Sharp and Ray Broomhill, *Short Changed: Women and Economic Policies*, Sydney: Allen and Unwin, 1988. For analysis of the impacts of global capitalism on women in developing countries see, for example, Barbara Ehrenreich and Arlie Russell Hochschild (editors), *Global Women: Nannies, Maids and Sex Workers in the*

New Economy, New York: Metropolitan Books, 2002. See also Lourdes Beneria, *Gender, Development and Globalization,* London: Routledge, 2003.

For more on the training and education debates from radical perspectives, see Thomas Dunk, Stephen McBride and Randle W. Nelsen (editors), *The Training Trap: Ideology, Training and the Labour Market,* Society for Socialist Studies and Fernwood Press, 1995–96.

The role of the capitalist state is analysed in Bob Jessop, *The Future of the Capitalist State,* London: Polity Press, 2002. The annual publication *The Socialist Register,* edited by Leo Panitch and Colin Leys, contains lively and informative radical perspectives on contemporary capitalism.

Notes

1 For further discussion see Heilbroner (2000: 120).

2 The term comes from Strange (1986).

3 See, for example, *The Socialist Register* 1999 which is entitled "Global Capitalism vs. Democracy".

4 See UNDP, Millennium Development Goals, available at www.undp.org.

5 Figures from National Center for Children in Poverty, Child Poverty Fact Sheet June 2001. Available at www.nccp.org. The data also show that 18 per cent of children under the age of six were living in poverty and 8 per cent in extreme poverty. The trend is rising, with 1.6 million more children living in poverty in 2001 than in 1979.

6 According to the UNAIDS/WHO, AIDS Epidemic Update December 2002, 29.4 million of the 42 million people living with HIV/AIDS are in sub-Saharan Africa. Globally, 3.1 million people died of HIV/AIDS in 2002 while 5 million people were newly infected.

7 Quoted in L. Garrett, 2000, *Betrayal of Trust: the Collapse of Global Public Health*, New York: Hyperion. I am grateful to Karine Peschard for bringing this quote to my attention.

8 See Carter (2001) for an extensive discussion of the critiques which are summarized in the next two paragraphs.

9 See, for example, the review provided in Sharp and Broomhill (1988).

10 See, for example, Elson and Pearson (1981).

11 See, for example, Standing (1989).

12 See Sian Powell, "W Papua mine paid $18.5m to military", *The Weekend Australian*, 15–16 March 2003, p. 19.

CHAPTER 4

Empire and crises
1870–1945

Capitalism unfolds

BY THE MID-EIGHTEENTH CENTURY, the economic and political organization of the world had been steadily and brutally transformed during the previous three centuries. Trade and mercantile activities had established a market interlinking parts of the world. The search for the sea passage to the Orient, facilitated by the changes in ship-building design and the invention of the compass, resulted in the "age of discovery" as adventurers from Europe – Vasco da Gama, John Cabot, James Cook and Christopher Columbus among others – "discovered" the Americas and the Pacific, plundering wealth as they went, destroying indigenous populations, and boosting the European nobility's material wealth in the process.[1] The great trading companies, such as the British and the Dutch East India Companies and the Hudson's Bay Company, were granted state monopolies in return for planting the flag in foreign lands. Africa provided the slaves for the new European colonies in the Americas.

It was against this historical backdrop that the process of capitalist industrialization began in Britain before spreading to continental Europe and North America. In Britain, an urban proletariat had been created by the enclosure movement – the removal of peasants from the land – and the factory system had emerged as a result of combining the productive power of labour with new inventions from the spinning jenny to steam power. Feudal structures broke down and the capitalist class was instrumental in shaping the state and state policy in its interests from extending the franchise, to regulations on commerce and the repression of workers' attempts to organize.

In 1848, Europe was gripped by revolution as workers fought back, but capitalism survived and expanded further. By 1870, Britain stood pre-eminent, producing one-third of the world's manufactured goods and accounting for one-quarter of world trade. Over the next 40 years both of these figures were to be roughly halved as other countries, in Europe but also the US, gained in relative economic strength.[2] The dynamics of this changing hierarchy were not, however, to be smooth politically or economically.

The curse of capitalism: late nineteenth-century crises

From 1873 until 1890, European countries experienced a prolonged depression. This led to social unrest and was accompanied by various financial crises across the capitalist world involving stock market crashes and bank failures. Michel Beaud (2001: 136–137) provides the following examples: the 1873 Vienna stock exchange crash which was followed by bank failures in

Austria and Germany; the 1882 stock exchange crash in Lyons followed by bank failures in France; the "railroad panic" in the US in 1884 and the associated bank failures, bankruptcies and wage reductions; the bankruptcy in 1889 of the Metals Company in France (and the company responsible for building the Panama Canal) and an ensuing stock exchange panic; the suspension of payments in 1890 by Baring Bros bank in England and the Bank of England's subsequent intervention to limit the banking panic; and the 1893 collapse in the stock prices for railroads in the US and the failure of 491 banks.

Capitalism's expansion during the mid- to late nineteenth century was accompanied by persistent cycles and crises which spread internationally among the rising capitalist powers. The response to this period of rapid technological change but also instability, illustrated by the instability of financial markets, was for industries to form cartels to protect themselves from market competition. These cartels were based on an alliance between industrial and financial interests. It was with this rise of "finance capital" that states extended their imperial ambitions as a way of supporting their own cartels' business interests.

Overseas expansion as the response to crises

All of the leading political economists of the period, from establishment figures such as John Stuart Mill to radical critics such as Vladimir Lenin, viewed capitalist economies as being subject to a falling rate of profit. It was seen as "natural", therefore, for capitalist economies to seek outlets overseas for capital investment where more profitable opportunities could be found. The result during this period was a rapid rise in the export of capital in search of new markets and new resources. The extension of Empire was viewed as an outcome of the workings of capitalism, even if it was enthusiastically proposed by some but criticized by others. As the historian D.K. Fieldhouse (1981: 2–3) points out, for some writers, such as Lenin, imperialism was seen as an inevitable outcome of the phase of monopoly capitalism, while for others Empire was seen as more of a choice, rather than an imperative, in which at least some countries could be described as "reluctant imperialists". Whether it was through reluctant choice or inevitability, imperialism was one of the historical outcomes of capitalism in this period.

China had been opened up by Britain's gunboat diplomacy in the 1840s, and in the 1850s the US had forced Japan to open its ports to Western commerce; India had already been brought under British jurisdiction in the late eighteenth century. In the mid- to late nineteenth century, the outlet for European powers searching for profitable markets and resources was primarily focused on Africa and Southeast Asia. Here, imperialism took the specific form of "colonialism" (Box 4.1).

BOX 4.1

Imperialism and colonialism

Imperialism refers to a process in which the interests of dominant countries are imposed on those of dominated countries. The polities and economies of the dominated countries are systematically restructured to serve the interests of the dominating countries. There are a broad range of mechanisms which can be used to foster imperialism and support empires. These mechanisms may be military threats and actions or the imposition of particular international "rules of the game" which benefit some countries. For example, it is common for left critics to refer to "free trade imperialism" – meaning the use of trade rules to benefit dominant countries. In all cases, imperialism refers to the use of state power to protect and promote the economic interests of its firms.

The motives for imperialism are often derived from the nature of capitalism. That is, imperialism results from the pursuit of profit on a worldwide scale. This was most famously argued in Lenin's classic, *Imperialism, the Highest Stage of Capitalism*, written in 1916. Others have viewed militarism, nationalism and racism, not capitalism *per se*, as the motives for imperialism.

Colonialism is one specific form of imperialism which describes the situation in which the imperial power directly administers the dominated country. As Fieldhouse (1981: 311) explains, colonialism "attempts to describe what proved to be a brief period and transient condition that was experienced by most parts of Africa, and much of South-east Asia and the Pacific, during the period 1870–1945 . . . Under colonialism a dependent society was totally controlled by the imperial power. Its government was in the hands of officials of the imperial state, its social, legal, educational, cultural and even religious life was moulded by alien hands and its economy was structured to meet the needs of European capitalism . . . Thus colonialism was merely one stage in the evolution of international relationships in the modern world whose central theme was the subordination of all countries to the needs of advanced capitalism."

The phenomenon of "colonialism" differentiates the period 1870–1945 from other episodes of Empire which had relied on colonization – the settling of lands by European inhabitants who sought to make "their" new countries resemble the old ones as much as possible – or on mechanisms for informal rule which relied on existing political structures, and the elites within them, to deliver the required benefits to the imperial powers.[3]

During this period the major imperial powers, principally Britain and France although also joined by Italy, Germany, the Netherlands, Belgium, the US and Japan, drew and redrew the maps of the world, literally through treaties and violently through war and conquest both with each other and with native populations. European and US national capitalisms, rooted in states and supported by them, searched the globe for markets and resources and incorporated larger and larger geographical areas in support of the insatiable pursuit of profit. As they did so, capitalism(s) emerged in the colonized countries as production was increasingly centred on international firms, and those serving them, on the basis of private property, the pursuit of profit and the employment of wage labour.

The expansion of the orbit of capitalism during this period, the conquest of new lands, the increase in capital flows and the rising economic interdependencies have led some writers to view this period of capitalist imperialism as a late nineteenth-century version of "globalization".

As the historian Niall Ferguson (2001: 6) notes, the result of this "globalization by force" was that "a small number of European countries governed an inordinately large amount of the rest of the world. On the eve of the First World War, Britain, France, Belgium, Holland and Germany – which between them accounted for around 0.9 per cent of the world's land surface and 7.5 per cent of its population – ruled in the region of 33 per cent of the rest of the world's area and 27 per cent of its people. All of Australasia, nearly all of Polynesia, 90 per cent of Africa and 56 per cent of Asia were under some form of European rule. And although only 27 per cent of the American continent – mainly Canada – found itself in the same condition, nearly all the rest had been ruled from Europe at one time or another in the seventeenth and eighteenth centuries."

As capitalism spread throughout the world during this period on the basis of colonial conquest, it did so, particularly in the British case, under the ideologies of "free trade" and "civilization". While private property was established and markets were opened up by colonial invasions, the prevailing economic orthodoxy was one of "free trade". In the 1840s, Britain officially adopted free trade as its policy, arguing that all countries should open their borders to trade with the world's first and, at the time, leading industrial nation. This ideology was followed by the Dutch and Belgian imperialists, but various degrees of protectionism remained in the other colonial trading systems.[4]

The benefits of free trade for all countries had been theorized by English political economist David Ricardo in the 1820s, but while Britain subsequently adopted this policy as its official policy, it was also accompanied by the belief that Empire was a good vehicle for economic advancement. And while the colonies could trade with whom they wished on a free trade basis, they were still colonies, ruled by a foreign power and open to its investors. "Free trade" meant opening up other countries' markets. To this economic agenda was added the arrogance of Western societies' belief in their own cultural and racial superiority so that Empire, rather than simply being viewed as a response to domestic economic problems, was often portrayed as a glorious "civilizing" mission. The ideals of capitalist democracy and the realities of capitalist imperialism sat uneasily together. The French Empire, for example, as Fieldhouse (1981: 36) has argued, was premised on direct rule and assimilation to French culture. But "a republic which believed in equality and representative government"

(Fieldhouse 1981: 37) allowed its colonial inhabitants only limited political freedoms.

Furthermore, while Britain preached free trade (and practised colonialism), other countries such as Germany and the US, pursuing industrialization after Britain, adopted policies which were more protectionist in nature. They relied on a variety of tariffs and controls to protect their own fledgling industries from competition from their more mature British competitors. According to the nineteenth-century German economist Friedrich List (1966), countries which were "late industrializers" required more extensive state involvement and direction in order to counteract the advantages enjoyed by the early industrializer. This became, as we will see in Chapter 5, an article of faith for the East and Southeast Asian "late, late industrializers" after 1945.

The economic rivalries between the main capitalist powers produced political rivalries as states built empires. As the historian Eric Hobsbawm has written (1994: 29), "In the Age of Empire, politics and economics had fused. International political rivalry was modelled on economic growth and competition, but the characteristic feature of this was precisely that it had no limit. The 'natural frontiers' of Standard Oil, the Deutsche Bank or the De Beers Diamond Company were at the end of the universe, or rather at the limits of their capacity to expand." International political rivalries led to war – the Great War of 1914–1918 (Box 4.2).

While some empires collapsed as a result of the First World War, others did not. By 1921, the British Empire was larger than ever. As one historian has commented, "in this system there lived some 450 million people, over one quarter of the human race. No contemporary empire, no previous empire, no subsequent

BOX 4.2

Capitalism, imperialism and war

The relationship between capitalism and war has long been a point of fierce debate between capitalism's supporters and radical critics. For the critics, capitalism's pursuit of profit leads firms to seek out profits everywhere. Supported by their states, this leads to rivalries between capitalist states. Containing these rivalries in peaceful ways is liable to periodic breakdown when rivalries are high, when particular markets or resources of high economic or strategic importance are at stake or when local interests threaten imperial control. In any of these situations, capitalist countries, especially imperial powers, may resort to war as a way of defending their interests. The US-led war on Iraq – a "war for oil" in the view of critics – is but the latest example.

Capitalism's supporters reject this argument and argue that capitalist states, especially democratic ones, have a predisposition to be peaceful. Aggressive territorial expansionism is more typically due to nationalism and not the result of capitalism. In fact, capitalism, by increasing trade and economic interdependence between countries, is more likely to encourage the non-violent settling of disputes. Furthermore, capitalist democracies have historically not fought each other; wars have been between capitalist democracies and totalitarian regimes (capitalist and socialist).

empire could compare with this."[5] In the next quarter-century, however, the capitalist world was to change again and experience another world war.

The end of the First World War brought prosperity to some countries, particularly the US, where the rich celebrated the "roaring 20s" in style. By 1929, national income in the US was over 40 per cent higher than it had been in 1919 and the US now accounted for nearly half of the world's industrial output.[6] The technological breakthrough of the internal combustion engine introduced a new consumer good – the automobile – which was to transform production methods, consumption patterns and the urban and rural landscapes of most countries for the rest of the century. Electricity generation increased and capitalism was characterized by what economist Joseph Schumpeter called waves of "creative destruction" – with the creativity of new technologies and products being accompanied by the destruction of other industries and processes. In short, capitalism was seen as a dynamic but unstable economic system.

Other countries, especially the countries of Europe, did not share in the dynamism and prosperity the US experienced during the 1920s. In Europe, the exhaustion of the First World War led to slower, halting and varied recoveries. Germany, weighed down with war reparations payments, was hard hit, with mounting unemployment after 1925. Britain also struggled. In fact, in Britain unemployment was over 10 per cent of the workforce for all of the 1920s.[7] Then came the 1930s.

The curse of capitalism: the Great Depression of the 1930s

The instability of the capitalist system was illustrated in all its force by the Great Depression of the 1930s. The US stock market had been rising spectacularly during the late 1920s, more than doubling its level between 1925 and 1929, as the economy boomed. However, the bubble well and truly burst with the Wall Street Crash of 1929. Over the next few years, bank failures and financial panics occurred throughout the major capitalist economies, and the international payments system broke down as country after country, including Britain and the US, were forced to abandon the Gold Standard. Deflation was passed from country to country as tariffs were raised, exchange rates were competitively devalued, and governments grimly stuck to their "sound finance", balanced budget policies.

The standard prescriptions – that the market would correct itself – were followed but with no reward. In the US, the excesses of the 1920s were seen as the cause of the Great Depression of the 1930s. For this reason, Treasury Secretary Andrew Mellon advised President Hoover to "liquidate labor, liquidate stocks, liquidate farmers, liquidate real estate".[8] The effect of this would be to "purge the rottenness out of the system. High costs of living will come down. People will work harder, live a more moral life. Values will be adjusted, and enterprising people will pick up the wrecks from less competent people."[9] As Parker dryly notes, "Hoover apparently followed this advice as the Depression wore on" (Parker 2002: 9). Meanwhile, un-employment in the US went from just over 3 per cent of the workforce in 1929 to over 25 per cent in 1933. And those who were not officially unemployed but were on the farms fared just as badly. In Germany, as Clavin (2000: 117) points out, "Bruning became known as the 'Hunger Chancellor' because he raised unemployment contributions, cut civil servants' pay and reduced the amount of taxation transferred by the central government to the state and local level."

A decade of economic misery followed for millions across the world as nations sought refuge in trade within their own borders (or extended borders including their colonial empires), as investment dried up in the face of excess capacity and low expectations of profit, and as international financial flows plummeted. The unemployed were told that they were responsible for their own situation for demanding wages which were too high.

The human cost: riding the rails, searching for work and the crime of vagrancy

Men were left to scour the country in search of non-existent jobs. "Riding the rails" became a way of life for single men in North America, until the state, regarding this mobile army of the unemployed as too dangerous for stability, outlawed the practice. In Canada, the single unemployed were given basic rations in return for military-supervised work. Personal accounts of the Depression tell of the suffering. Louis Banks described his experience in the US: "I was in a chain gang in Georgia. I had to pick cotton four months, just for hoboin' on a train. Just for vag."[10] When he had served his sentence he was given 35 cents for his four months' work. Charles Graham recalls his days during the Depression in South Shields, UK: "Usually we had a slice a bread in the morning. For dinner a penn'orth of each, that's a penn'orth of fish and a penn'orth of chips; and probably a couple slices of bread at night. That was the staple diet of the average person . . . I was a prisoner of war for two-and-a-half years and I think I got through it pretty easy because it was similar in a sense. We weren't entitled to school dinners. There was people in a much worse plight than we."[11] Jimmy Buckley recalls returning from his honeymoon to find his new life shattered by the sign "THIS MILL HAS CLOSED DOWN INDEFINITELY". He explains: "It was awful going out every morning looking for work. It was fruitless. I used to go six or seven miles each morning on my bicycle and there'd be nothing. My mill never opened again. Spinning just died out."[12] Half a world away, the cotton mills of India were also closing. And, as Rothermund (1992: 79–80) points out, Indian peasant farmers were faced with ruin as agricultural prices fell by a half within a few months but their debts and rent payments remained unchanged. Land was forcibly sold and tenancies were ended.

While working-class men were searching for non-existent work, the experiences of working-class women during the Depression were mixed. For example, economic historian Patricia Clavin (2000: 113) notes that "in some countries new legislation was enacted to force women from the workplace. Steps taken in the Weimar Republic [of Germany] to discriminate against so-called 'double earners', married women whose husbands were expected to bring in a 'family wage', is a good example. At the same time, there are also cases where employers preferred to sack the males and keep their female workers because they were cheaper." The complex interactions between capitalism and patriarchy led to women experiencing the Depression in a variety of ways.

Despite the prevailing economic orthodoxy and political ideology which sought to cast the blame for the Depression at the feet of the workers and which therefore sought to cut their wages, it was a blame which many refused to accept. Strikes, including general strikes and frequently violent, were common in many capitalist countries during the 1920s and the first half of the 1930s as workers acted in solidarity to oppose employers cutting their wages and to press governments to accept some responsibility for the economic malaise in the countries which they governed.

National responses to the Depression: Swedish social democracy, the "New Deal" in the US and the spread of fascism in Europe

The "New Deal" was launched by President Roosevelt in the US, and in Sweden the social democratic welfare state was launched as a political project in the 1930s. At any rate, the philosophy of government's role in the economy was beginning to change but only slowly. Indeed, as Garside (1993: 5) observes, "the balance of interest group power in Britain was not fundamentally shaken by the Depression, permitting policy to be Treasury-dominated down to 1938 and beyond". The ideas of Keynes, the major intellectual opponent of "the Treasury view" that there was "no alternative" to conservative economic policies, were to be more important in shaping post-1945 policy than they were in the inter-war years.

Elsewhere in Europe, other forms of national programmes to deal with the Depression emerged. The failure of the capitalist powers to repair the international apparatus governing their economic relations led increasingly to the adoption of national solutions. While the limited welfarism of Roosevelt was adopted in the US, Franco, Hitler and Mussolini led Spain, Germany and Italy down the path to fascism. Japan followed the latter route too. In these countries trade unions were banned, labour was subordinated to the needs of large corporations and, to varying degrees, the autonomy of big business was challenged by the state. The Great Depression inevitably spread its economic and political turmoil beyond the capitalist core. As Hobsbawm (1994: 104) notes, in Latin America "twelve countries changed government or regime in 1930–31, ten of them by military coup". In India, Gandhi's nationalist movement gained strength.

None of the national programmes of the capitalist core met with sustained economic success. In Clavin's view (2000: 168), "in 1937 the world economy turned down once more and, had it not been for war preparations, a new depression would have engulfed the European economy at the end of the decade". A second Great Depression among the capitalist powers was therefore averted but only by a militarism which culminated in another "Great War" and which was fought at staggering human costs. Some 57 million, or 2.4 per cent of the world's population, are estimated to have died in the Second World War.[13]

The heaviest cost, in terms of lost lives, was borne by the Soviet Union. This new actor on the international stage signalled a dramatic reverse in the global reach of capitalism. The uninterrupted global expansion of capitalism, in evidence from the seventeenth to the nineteenth centuries, had begun to be challenged. For the first time, as the result of the Russian revolution in 1917, a significant part of the European landmass was removed from capitalism's orbit, a trend which was to be evident worldwide after 1945. A state socialist alternative to the ravages of capitalism appeared to be viable.

That alternatives to capitalism were sought is easy to understand in view of the history of capitalism reviewed in this chapter. "Actually existing capitalism" bore little resemblance to the "natural and free" system theorized by its proponents. Markets and private property were not "naturally" developed in many parts of the world but were forced upon foreign lands as a result of imperial ambitions. The pursuit of profit led to territorial expansion and national rivalries in the period up to 1914.

Capitalist rivalries led to an imperial war. For some critics, it was war that was a "natural" outcome of capitalism. If capitalism resulted in "freedom", it did so for the large private firms supporting the Empire and not for the millions of colonial subjects. And for many workers in the 1930s, their only "freedom" was the freedom to get on their bikes and look for work; they were not free, however, to look by train.

The picture of capitalism as an unjust and unstable system finds much compelling support. Capitalism during this whole period was plagued by instability. Financial crises and bank failures were routine events. Economic hardship was a way of life for many, even in the capitalist heartlands of Europe and North America. Some made spectacular fortunes as the Carnegies, the Fords and the Rockefellers testify. But even the middle class did well at the expense of the misery of the unemployed. As David Rossman, a psychiatrist in the US, remembers, "you could get the most wonderful kind of help for a pittance. People would work for next to nothing. That's when people were peddling apples and bread lines were forming all over the city."[14] The apple peddlers were subject to continual economic insecurity amid rudimentary welfare systems and were viewed as the architects of their own demise. Messianic fascist leaders promised order out of chaos but delivered only intolerance, brutality and, finally, carnage.

Perhaps unsurprisingly, the traumas of the first half of the twentieth century led the major capitalist victors, the US and the UK, to design an institutional framework for the post-1945 world aimed at ensuring that the destructive and disruptive tendencies of capitalism would be effectively banished. The Bretton Woods agreement of 1944 set up the post-war capitalist world's international order. This agreement sought to provide national governments with the tools necessary to pursue policies of full employment domestically and to create the international institutions capable of ensuring that adjustments between countries were handled effectively and fairly. There would be no repeats of the beggar-thy-neighbour policies of the 1930s and no retreats into autarchy or competing regional blocs. This was to be a well-regulated international system, underwritten by, and based upon the power of, the world's leading capitalist power, the US. Within this framework, national policies to reduce economic insecurity could be implemented. For this reason, while trade flows were facilitated and encouraged, capital flows between countries were regulated to permit national governments some autonomy in setting and meeting their own national policy objectives.

Two international financial institutions, the International Monetary Fund (IMF) and the International Bank for Reconstruction and Development (IBRD or World Bank), were set up. The IMF was charged with ensuring that countries experiencing short-term balance of payments problems could obtain sufficient liquidity to enable them to take necessary corrective measures without undue hardship. And the World Bank was set up to provide long-term credit for financing economic development, focused initially on the reconstruction of war-torn Europe but soon afterwards on the capitalist developing countries.

Perhaps surprisingly, in view of the history of capitalism in the pre-1945 period, the capitalist system went through a remarkable metamorphosis and the two decades following the end of the Second World War were ones of unprecedented prosperity and stability in capitalist countries. A reformed capitalism, based on Keynesianism, offered a more humane and stable capitalism in sharp contrast to its pre-1945 incarnation. How the next half-century of capitalism unfolded is the subject of the following two chapters.

Further reading

For a good introduction to radical theories of imperialism see Anthony Brewer, *Marxist Theories of Imperialism: A Critical Survey*, New York: Routledge, 1990. D.K. Fieldhouse's *Colonialism 1870–1945: An Introduction* provides an excellent account of the subject. For the role of imperialism in spreading capitalism to developing countries, see Bill Warren, *Imperialism: Pioneer of Capitalism*, London: Verso, 1980. Gordon Martel's, *The Origins of the First World War*, London: Longman, 1996, provides an accessible and lucid discussion of the pre-1914 period and, within this historical context, outlines the various positions on relationships between imperialism, nationalism and war.

The relationships between free trade and Empire were complex in late nineteenth-century Britain. Some free traders hoped that free trade would lead to the dissolution of Empire, while anti-free traders argued that imperial preferences be used to protect the Empire from unfair competition by other non-free-trading imperial powers. The official policy for much of this period, however, was free trade and Empire. The various positions are set out well in Jim Tomlinson, *Problems of British Economic Policy, 1870–1945*, London: Methuen, 1981, Chapter 3.

There are many excellent histories of the period. I like Eric Hobsbawm's companion volumes *The Age of Empire 1875–1914*, London: Cardinal, 1989 and *Age of Extremes: The Short Twentieth Century 1914–1991*, London: Michael Joseph, 1994. The latter places a good deal of emphasis on the rivalry between capitalism and (Soviet) socialism. For the 1930s, Patricia Clavin's *The Great Depression in Europe 1929–1939*, Basingstoke: Macmillan, 2000, provides a thorough economic history. Personal accounts of the Depression can be found in Studs Terkel, *Hard Times: An Oral History of the Great Depression*, London: Allen Lane, The Penguin Press, 1970 and Nigel Gray, *The Worst of Times: An Oral History of the Great Depression in Britain*, Totowa, NJ: Barnes and Noble, 1985. George Orwell's *The Road to Wigan Pier*, London: Secker and Warburg, 1998, is also worth reading to get a sense of the period.

Notes

1 Robbins (2002: 73) reports that "in all, it is estimated that 95–98 percent of the indigenous population of the Americas died as a consequence of European contact" through military combat, slavery and, most importantly, disease.

2 Data drawn from Kennedy (1983a: 92).

3 See Fieldhouse (1981) for discussion.

4 See Fieldhouse (1981: 56–57) for more details.

5 Kennedy (1983b: 199).

6 See Parker (2002: 2).

7 Clavin (2000: 75).

8 As quoted in Parker (2002: 9).

9 *Ibid.*

10 As quoted in Terkel (1970: 41).

11 As quoted in Gray (1985: 91–92).

12 As quoted in Gray (1985: 154–155).

13 Ferguson (2001: 9).

14 As quoted in Terkel (1970: 80).

CHAPTER 5

Post-1945 capitalism: variations across countries

National capitalisms

A COHERENT SET OF INSTITUTIONS and mechanisms were set up after 1945 to regulate capitalism at the international level. This still left substantial room, however, for a number of distinct varieties of national capitalism. In part, this was because the initial design of the Bretton Woods system, with its restrictions on international capital flows, allowed considerable scope for economic policy autonomy at the national level. But the existence of national varieties of capitalism goes well beyond this scope for policy autonomy and reflects wider and more profound differences in the practice of capitalism around the world.

Variations in national capitalisms, in general, can be attributed to the fact that economies are path-dependent, that is, they have histories which shape the decisions which are made and the institutions which arise, in any particular time period. These histories include the strength of various classes, the national experiences which countries have been through and the challenges which they face. "Markets" do not exist in institutional vacuums but, as sociologists such as Karl Polanyi (1944) have argued, are "embedded" in social structures. How markets operate depends, therefore, on how national capitalist economies have been forged and evolved.

Furthermore, many of the actors in capitalist economies – governments, firms and associations – function in ways which do not rely on "the market". Boyer and Hollingsworth (1997: 433), for example, two authors who stress the social and institutional framework within which economic activity takes place, argue that "some of the most competitive firms, regions, and nations are based on mechanisms of economic coordination that are totally different from pure market mechanisms". These methods of coordination range from internal hierarchies in case of the firms, to high levels of trust and cooperation (or social capital) for regions and nations, and to market-guiding government intervention at the national level. They all point to the need to consider the wider social, political and organizational structures within which capitalist profit-making takes place.

In the post-1945 period national capitalisms also varied because of the different specific challenges which they faced. The defeated countries of Japan and Germany faced a different set of challenges than the victorious powers. The Allied occupation of Japan in the immediate post-war period led to the adoption of a new constitution. Germany's fear of a repeat of the hyper-inflation of the early 1930s was reflected in a strong role for a conservative Bundesbank. The history of colonialism in the

Third World led to nationalist movements in the post-1945 period, movements which sought independence and national control over their economies.

Of course, capitalist countries also faced many similar challenges. For example, it was clear in all of the advanced core capitalist countries that new institutional arrangements would be required to ensure that the demands of a stronger labour movement could be accommodated. Capitalism would need to be reformed to address labour's calls for greater economic security and a fairer distribution of income. In the core countries, the power of the organized working class and the extension of the franchise, while growing throughout the century, had by the end of the Second World War become sufficiently widespread that it was necessary for labour to be more fully incorporated into economic decision-making. Labour, at least in the core countries, had become a political force which could no longer be ignored or suppressed.

All capitalist countries were also left with the legacy of the devastation of the previous 50 years, a legacy which brought a determination and general acceptance of the need to find a more humane operational basis for capitalism. This was based not only on the experience of the 1930s but also on a necessity to meet the challenge posed by a rising Soviet Union offering a non-capitalist alternative. But the institutions which emerged in the face of these common challenges showed considerable variation between countries. A number of national capitalisms became evident as each country addressed the historical legacies and post-war challenges in different ways.

Most of the analyses of different varieties of national capitalism have focused on the core capitalist countries, especially on the US, UK, Germany, Japan and the Scandinavian countries. I follow this convention here and first summarize the types of capitalism, drawing primarily on these countries. These varieties of capitalism are sometimes referred to as "models" of capitalism. This points to the fact that these national capitalisms can be seen as coherent sets of institutions which can be theorized at the abstract level. Following the overview of the versions or "models" of capitalism found in the core capitalist countries, I will also briefly discuss some of the other varieties of capitalism which have been found outside of the capitalist core.

How capitalisms differ: state–capital–labour relations

National capitalisms can be differentiated by the nature of the relations between the main agents in the economy, namely, the state, capital (itself sometimes divided between finance and industry) and labour. That is, national capitalisms can be differentiated by the ways in which state–capital–labour relations are organized. In some analyses, the distinctions between capitalisms are analysed in terms of variations in "state–market" relations, where the market referred to here consists of the actions of businesses and, with less frequency, the actions of labour.

Consider first, state–capital (or state–business) relations. These relations vary depending on the role assigned to the state in managing the economy. One model is for the state to be responsible for the macroeconomy but to play no direct or guiding role in the decisions taken by firms as to how much they should invest or in what fields to invest. A different approach is for the government to play a much larger direct or indirect role in ensuring adequate levels of private investment and perhaps playing a role in the allocation of that investment to certain key industrial sectors, such as the microelectronics or heavy industry sectors, for example.

Secondly, how should capital–labour relations be managed? One model is for the state to provide the legal framework within which firms and trade unions must operate but, having provided this, to play little further role in determining the outcome of wage bargaining. In this approach, wage bargaining takes place in a decentralized fashion with the outcomes determined by the relative strengths of firms and unions in particular industries. A different approach is for the state, as well as providing a legal framework for the conduct of industrial relations, to take an active role in determining the level of wage settlements in the economy. This approach relies upon the government, employers and trade unions negotiating at the national level about what the economy can afford, how much will be distributed as wages and profits, and how much the government will provide in terms of welfare state provisions or the "social wage". Often referred to as "corporatism", this model relies on a more consensual form of capitalism.[1] It also points to a further way of distinguishing between national capitalisms – on the basis of the extent and forms of welfare states. A final "model" is for the state to actively impose forms of labour organization, and roles for trade unions, which seek to control the power of organized labour.

A further issue relating to capital–labour relations concerns how training is organized and who is responsible for it. If labour is, or is encouraged to be, mobile between firms, then any individual firm has little incentive to incur the cost of training workers. If it does so, it will pay the costs of training but the worker may subsequently be poached by other firms who are able to offer higher wages precisely because they do not incur training costs themselves. In such a situation, firms are penalized if they provide training and the level of investment in workers in the economy is likely to be low. In this case, the state may step in to provide the training that firms would like but are unlikely to provide themselves. In other economies, workers may, through various incentives and mechanisms, be encouraged to stay with firms for a long period, perhaps even a lifetime of employment. In these circumstances, it is much more obviously in the firms' interests to provide worker training.

A third factor differentiating national capitalisms concerns the ways in which industry is financed. In this context, a distinction is typically made between stock market and bank based systems of industrial financing. In stock market based systems, firms raise their external funds through the issue of equities as well as through bank loans. Stock markets are therefore used as an intermediary between savers (individuals and institutional investors) and borrowers (the firms). The expected profitability of the firm is reflected in the stock market price and the manager of the firm is required to maximize profits in order to maximize the returns to shareholders. In this way, it is argued that stock markets discipline firm executives to act in the interests of the shareholders (rather their in their own interests); if they don't, share prices will fall and shareholders may replace the existing executives with more competent or profit-oriented executives. If executives are not utilizing the firm's resources efficiently, they also run the threat of being taken over by other firms who see an opportunity to reorganize production and increase profits. In theory, this is the role that stock markets play in capitalist economies.

Critics of the stock market based financial system argue that shareholders actually have very little oversight over firm executives; the latter frequently get huge salaries and bonuses despite the poor performance of their firms. Critics also argue that this system leads to "short-termism" where firm executives have to focus on short-term share prices and takeover threats to the detriment of long-run strategic planning and investment. The latter, it is argued, is best realized in a bank based financial system in which banks are the main lenders to firms. Banks, the argument runs, can use their expertise to better evaluate firm investment plans and, by developing long-term relationships with firms often including a seat on the firm's board, can provide long-term support for soundly managed firms. Opponents of this system argue that it can lead to bank–business relations becoming too close with the result that independent financial decisions are compromised, and that this model tends to disadvantage new firms entering the market.

Given these dimensions over which national capitalisms may vary, sumarized in Box 5.1, it is common to find a number of different types of capitalism identified among the major capitalist countries. Typically, between two and four varieties of capitalism are identified, with the membership of each variety depending on the precise features of capitalism under investigation.

Here, I distinguish between three broad types of capitalism. It should be remembered that these types are generalizations which seek to capture the basic features of particular countries, although important differences are still likely to remain even between countries which are members of the same type. The three types are the Anglo-American (or *laissez-faire* or liberal) model, the northern European (or corporatist) model, and the Japanese (or developmentalist) model.

BOX 5.1

How national capitalisms differ

1 In state–capital relations by the degree to which governments (or state agencies) directly intervene or guide investment decisions.

2 In state–capital–labour relations by the degree to which governments are involved in wage determination.

3 In state–labour relations by the extent and form of the welfare state (or the social wage).

4 In state–labour relations by the degree of state control over labour organizations and trade unions.

5 In state–capital–labour relations in terms of who provides training.

6 In industry–finance relations in terms of the relative importance of banks and stock markets in financing firms' investment.

The Anglo-American model: decentralized wage bargaining and stock markets

The Anglo-American model, based on the experience and institutional frameworks of capitalism in the US and the UK, has the following characteristics. It is a decentralized system in which wage bargaining is conducted without the direct intervention of the state. Capital–labour relations are conceived in basically adversarial terms and strikes are a normal part of industrial bargaining. The state provides, and often changes, the legal framework within which bargaining takes place. The changes in the legal framework may be intended to strengthen the bargaining hand of one of the agents, capital or labour, at the expense of the other and, as a result, may be resisted from time to time by those disadvantaged. Labour markets are relatively "thick" in the sense that workers may move relatively freely between firms. Long-term contracts are relatively uncommon, with firms more likely to adjust to changes in demand by laying off workers, and firm investment in worker training is relatively low. This model is also characterized by a relatively high reliance on stock markets as financial intermediaries. The welfare state does not enter as part of an explicit bargain over a "social wage" but has a more residual form, especially in the US, where it has been designed to serve as a protection against poverty and as a safety net rather than as a more extensive vehicle aimed at promoting egalitarian outcomes. In the UK the welfare state played a more extensive role, especially in the 1945–1979 period; the US has been much closer to a low tax–low welfare state model. This Anglo-American model of capitalism gives a large coordinating role to markets and assigns a relatively small direct role to the state.

The northern European or corporatist model: consensual decision-making and a large welfare state

The northern European or corporatist model is typically attributed to countries such as Germany, Sweden and Norway and sometimes includes other countries such as Denmark and Belgium. These countries have developed a form of capitalism in which wage bargaining takes place at the national level typically between representatives of capital, labour and the state. The national bargaining framework also covers welfare state services and income distribution objectives. This is a high tax–high welfare state model. Tripartite committees, between capital, labour and the state, form an important part of the overall policy framework. Workplace industrial relations have attempted to follow a more cooperative path, and industrial democracy, including having workers' representatives on company boards, has been given a higher profile in this model. Relations between employer and employee have been more stable, based on longer-term commitments and institutionalized through employment protection. Finance is primarily bank-based with long-term relationships established between banks and firms to whom they lend. Thus, this model is characterized by "patient capital" and "patient labour", to use German economist Wolfgang Streeck's (2001) terms. The compromise between capital and labour under this form of capitalism therefore differs substantially from the compromise reached in the case of Anglo-American capitalism. In the European corporatist model, capital and labour appear more as partners with the state in national economic planning. In the Anglo-American model, the state takes a back seat and independent capital and labour organizations confront each other in more adversarial terms.

An aside on varieties of welfare states

The classification of countries into different "varieties" changes depending on the issue being examined. I have classified countries according to state–capital–labour relations. In work focusing on the welfare state, however, Esping-Andersen (1990) proposes a division between liberal welfare states (as found in the US and

UK, for example), conservative/corporativistic welfare states (such as that found in Germany) and social democratic welfare states (as found in Norway and Sweden). In my analysis I have collapsed the latter two categories into one, since I am working at a more general level than a focus on the welfare state.

It is also worth noting that forms of the welfare state, since they influence the ways in which individuals and households relate to "the market", have implications for gender relations. Feminist analysis has differentiated between Esping-Andersen's "three worlds of welfare capitalism" on the basis of their implications for women. Ray Broomhill and Rhonda Sharp (2003) neatly summarize the implications in the following way. The liberal welfare state promotes a "dual breadwinner–female carer" gender contract in which women are expected to contribute to family income but to remain as primary care givers. In the conservative welfare state, policies have been structured to promote a "male breadwinner–female carer" gender contract in which more support is given to women to remain within the household. In the social democratic welfare state, a "dual breadwinner–state carer" gender contract has emerged in which policies are designed to permit a more equal sharing of work responsibilities but with substantial publicly funded caring. Varieties of welfare state, therefore, have important implications for gender relations.

Japanese (or East Asian) developmental capitalism: guiding the market and controlling labour

Corporatism finds resonance with the experience of the third variety of capitalism, national developmental capitalism, which is associated with the Japanese model. Here too, bank based finance dominates, with the *keiretsu* model – one bank with a set of client enterprises – being the preferred model for organizing the financing of investment. Long-term relationships between banks and firms are mirrored by long-term relationships between firms – such as suppliers with their purchasers – and between firms with their employees. Indeed, until very recently, "lifetime employment" was the norm for large Japanese firms. Under these circumstances, labour mobility between firms was low and loyalty to the company was high. While these character-istics of the Japanese system demonstrate a commonality with the corporatist countries of northern Europe, other parts of the Japanese institutional framework depart from the northern European experience. This is particularly the case with respect to the role of labour. In Japan, trade unions were set up in 1945 under allied occupation, and a period of brutal and bloody strikes occurred during the next 15 years, culminating in the miners' strike of 1960. This was something of a watershed in Japanese industrial relations and after that a more consensual approach to industrial relations was implemented. In this system, unions were enterprise unions, that is, formed to represent the workers in one firm. This reduced the power of organized labour as a national force and led to a changed system of industrial relations in which company interests and worker interests were increas-ingly seen as overlapping.

The company formed a "mini-society" with workers increas-ingly identifying with "their" firm. A more egalitarian structure was encouraged with differences between shop floor workers and executives minimized (at least compared to the Anglo-American model). Pay scales reflected seniority as individuals were rewarded for length of service with the firm. Union leaders frequently became members of the management. It should be noted, however, that this structure was only relevant for large companies in Japan. In the small business sector, these practices were not found and a much less "cooperative" framework existed here.

While the Japanese model has some important similarities with the northern European corporatist countries in terms of the more consensual approach taken to economic management and industrial relations, there were also some distinctive characteristics. These distinctive characteristics can also be found in other areas. For example, the welfare state is much smaller in Japan than in European countries. Welfare provision is more likely to be provided and organized at the family or company level than at the state level. Women's participation in the workforce is lower than in many other OECD countries and the gender wage-gap, that is, the difference between the average wages of men and women, is typically higher than those found elsewhere.

Japan is also distinctive in the extent to which government agencies influenced the investment decisions of private corporations. The Ministry of International Trade and Industry (MITI) has been singled out by many authors for its key role in guiding the investment of Japanese companies into microelectronics and computers in the 1960s and 1970s. State policies towards foreign direct investment, international trade, finance and technology acquisition were all critical in building up Japan's own industrial base, protecting it from foreign competitors and fostering its entry into global markets.

It is this state-led development strategy, characterized by state control or influence over finance, technology and trade, which has led to the identification of a "Japanese model of capit-alist development" followed by Japan in the decades following the end of the Second World War and then adopted by other East Asian economies such as Taiwan and South Korea from the mid-1960s. In line with the writings of Friedrich List and the earlier experience of Germany and the US, these "late, late industrial-izers" relied on a model of capitalism which involved a greater role for the state. This interpretation of the characteristics of capitalist development in key East Asian countries provides an alternative to that of Fukuyama (1992) outlined in Chapter 2. State–capital relations were such that in the case of South Korea, for example, economist Alice Amsden (1989) has argued that the giant South Korean firms (or *chaebols* such as Samsung and Hyundai) were disciplined by state agencies. These firms would receive financial support from the state-controlled banking system only if they met export (or other) targets set by the government. This Japanese or East Asian developmentalist model also relied on a form of state–labour relations which was inimical to the existence of independent trade unions for a significant part of the period of capitalist industrialization. The limited role of the welfare state, greater reliance on the family, and more unequal conditions of work for women were also common throughout the East Asian countries.

These three varieties of capitalism – Anglo-American, northern European and Japanese developmentalist – have received consid-erable attention. These varieties describe capitalism in some, but not all, of the core capitalist countries. France, for example, does not fit neatly into any of these three varieties, and would con-stitute a fourth variety of national capitalism based on high levels of state planning but with less well-developed corporatist institutions than the northern European countries.

National varieties of capitalism as rivals

One question which is frequently asked is "Which variety of capitalism performs best?" "Best" is typically defined in terms of securing economic growth, full employment and distributional equity. This is a difficult question because describing institutional structures and measuring economic outcomes is easier to do than to establish causal relationships between them. Furthermore, the relative performance of the different types of capitalist model has also varied over time. In the 1960s, the 1970s and much of the 1980s, the growth of the Japanese, German and Scandinavian countries pointed to the superiority of these models. Faced with the turbulent decade of the 1970s when oil prices rose twice, it was argued that the corporatist countries were better able to adjust to these shocks because they had the institutional mechanisms in place which enabled societies to respond in relatively non-conflictual ways. In contrast, the UK was unable to effectively respond to the crises with its decentralized system of wage bargaining and its antagonistic industrial relations system. The US was argued to be in continual relative decline, with Japan, especially, increasingly challenging its economic predominance. Particularly in the 1980s and early 1990s, it was common to find books and articles on the Japanese "challenge", or more colourfully "threat", to the US and on predictions of economic "battles" and "wars" between the US and Japan. During this period, too, there was much talk of a coming "Pacific century" in which the centre of gravity of global capitalism would shift from the Atlantic to the Pacific or from the US to Asia. In short, the varieties of national capitalism were interpreted not simply as being interesting institutional frameworks for analysis but as rival capitalisms.

For much of the post-war period it seemed, therefore, that the corporatist or Japanese models would predominate in this struggle between rival forms of capitalism. However, in the 1990s, the relative performance of the US and UK provided a counter to this prediction. In the 1990s, the US economy enjoyed its longest post-war boom and the UK shed its label of being the "sick man of Europe". In contrast, Japan entered a decade-long slump and European growth rates slowed as the centralized wage bargaining system and extensive welfare state provision were seen as detrimental to economic and social "flexibility". The changes in the performance of national capitalisms over time are explored further in the next chapter.

Varieties of capitalism: a matter of choice or history?

Can a country choose to adopt the institutional framework of a different type of capitalism or are there historical and cultural constraints which limit the degree of choice? Certainly, popular commentators such as Will Hutton (2002), in arguing for Britain to become more similar to the northern European model, and less like the US, believe that institutional frameworks are transferable and adaptation is possible. Indeed, there have been a number of examples in the post-1945 period of countries attempting to adopt the institutional features of other models. For example, "Japanese-style" industrial relations have been introduced into "Anglo-American" settings, especially in the automobile industry. As another example, at the state level, Australia finds most resonance with the Anglo-American model but in the 1980s the Australian Labor Party introduced an "Accord" as a way of promoting more corporatist frameworks into the predominantly Anglo-American institutional setting. This experiment was problematic in that, lacking the deeper institutional foundations of corporatist countries, it often involved wage restraint on the part of labour but with little corresponding restraint on business (other than some form of "price restraint"). More often than not it collapsed into an unworkable "incomes policy" rather than being a genuine tool of social reform which changed the balance of power between capital, state and labour.[2] The same could be said of the "Social Contract" introduced by the British Labour Party in the 1970s.

The difficulties of transplanting the features of one variety of capitalism into another would not come as a surprise to those who point to the long historical roots of national capitalisms. They suggest a more cautious approach to the question of transferability. For example, the more interventionist, market constraining, variants of capitalism found in Germany and Japan have been argued to owe their origins to the industrialization process in these countries in the late nineteenth century. In the German case, Gerhard Lehmbruch (2001) argues that responses to the financial crises of the 1870s resulted in a sharing of state–private responsibilities which laid the basis for the subsequent development of corporatism. The importance of history is reinforced by Philip Manow (2001) who argues that the welfare state in Germany was developed in the late nineteenth century as a way of extending benefits to influential groups so as to secure their commitment to the dominant system in the absence of political democracy. The welfare state was subsequently expanded on more universalist principles in the post-1945 period.

Manow (2001) further argues that the enterprise-based welfare system developed in Japan also dates from the late nineteenth century and resulted from the same pressures to provide benefits to key constituencies in the absence of political democracy. In the Anglo-American cases, welfare states were more a response to the rising power of labour and class struggle "from below" rather than from "top-down" conservative reformers trying to engineer social peace and cooperation as in the German and Japanese cases (see Streeck 2001: 13). These examples, by illustrating that state–capital–labour relations have evolved over decades (and even centuries) within specific national contexts, suggest that the scope for "model choice" may be constrained in important ways. The prospects for a "convergence" of national capitalisms under the forces of globalization are discussed further in Chapter 7.

Varieties of capitalism: Asia, Russia and Latin America

Capitalism varies between the core capitalist countries, between non-core countries, and between the core and non-core countries. The state-led developmental capitalism of some of the countries of East Asia can also be seen as a form of "authoritarian capitalism", given the suppression of independent labour movements which has characterized the growth process in these countries. This variety of capitalism is not, however, the only way in which "Asian" capitalism has been described. Another popular interpretation places the emphasis on the role of "networks", particularly networks among the overseas Chinese diaspora. According to this interpretation, a unique brand of "Asian" or "Chinese" capitalism can be identified which relies heavily on personal relations and personal networks. "Markets", as arm's-length transactions between buyers and sellers who typically do not know each other, are less important in this model than personal contacts between participants who may be known to each other or connected through kinship or ethnic ties. These personal relations build levels of trust between agents in the economy which enable them to engage in transactions even where the security of private property or transparent regulation of the market is absent. Because of the role of kinship relations in these networks, and the role of the Chinese family-run business as the unit of production, this model is also sometimes referred to as being a "familial capitalism".

As a further variant, consider the capitalism that has emerged in Russia since the fall of communism. Here, the transition to capitalism occurred rapidly with the fall of Gorbachev in 1991. In came the IMF and Western economic advisors who proposed "shock therapy" to rapidly break the psychology of central planning and dependency on the state and to promote the "spontaneous" formation of markets. This, together with mass privatization, was to be the basis for capitalism. Bertram Silverman and Murray Yanowitch (2000: 128), in their study of the "New Russia", have argued that "unlike other capitalist countries, Russia started its transition to a modern market system as a state-controlled industrial economy and not as an economy characterized by early unbridled capitalism. Rather than humanizing an already existing capitalist system by increasing the role of government, trade unions, and other voluntary associations, Russia needed to dismantle its state-controlled economy and replace it with a modern mixed economy." However, in the process of dismantling state control, the reforms destroyed institutional government structures and resulted in "the disintegration of the social order" (Silverman and Yanowitch 2000: 130). The state apparatus was weakened to the point where it could not operate as an effective check on business – indeed it became subservient to its aims and was easily corrupted as the lines between private and public spheres became increasingly blurred. The result was therefore a transition to what has been referred to earlier as "gangster capitalism" with businesses able to operate largely above the law. The result for the Russian people has been growing poverty so that anywhere from 30 to 50 per cent of the population are now reported to be living below the poverty line (with women disproportionately represented), huge inequalities between the new rich capitalist elite (often members of the previous communist bureaucracy) and ordinary people, growing social problems, and plummeting male life expectancy. The Russian people have also had to cope with a collapse in output worse than that experienced in Western Europe in the Great Depression of the 1930s. The Russian "model" of capitalism, therefore, has blurred the lines between state and capital and largely excluded labour altogether as a political force.

In Latin America, differentiating models of capitalism is more problematic than in the core capitalist countries. For one thing, as John Sheahan (2002: 25) notes, in Latin America "countries change their versions of capitalism more frequently, and more radically, than European countries do". Furthermore, the political landscape is more complex, with military and/or authoritarian rule commonplace over the past half-century. As Sheahan argues (2002: 48), "Latin American capitalists have not been consistent enthusiasts for democracy. Nor have North American investors in the region."

Nevertheless, Sheahan suggests that two types of capitalism can be identified, although each has three sub-versions. The two broad versions are termed "liberal capitalism" (which corresponds most closely to the Anglo-American version discussed above) and a more "activist" version which stresses a greater economic role for the state in fostering development. Although there are some exceptions, the role of labour in Latin American capitalism is generally much weaker than in the core countries and is often repressed. One variant of the activist model allows for a more inclusionary political economy which typically provides greater opportunities for education than in other versions. The instability of regimes in the region has meant that many countries have, during the post-war period, experimented with several versions of capitalism, switching between liberal and activist versions and their sub-variants.

In Latin America, at least, governments have viewed alternative models of capitalism as policy choices. There remains some commonality between most of the experiments, however, in that patterns of landholding and income distribution are highly unequal and political power has remained concentrated in the hands of those closely allied to the holders of economic power, whether domestic or international.[3] As a result, poverty remains high, and by the end of the 1990s over half of the population of Latin America was living in poverty.[4]

State–capital relations in both Russia and, for most of the post-war period, much of Latin America can be characterized, therefore, as the state being the servant of the capital (and far removed from the imagined "impartial umpire" of the "ordered brawl"). It is not surprising to find many instances of corruption here as political leaders sought to enrich themselves in the process of ensuring that private firms were provided with a "favourable business environment". In other countries outside the core – the Philippines under Marcos and Zaïre (the Congo) under Mobutu come readily to mind – the state was powerful enough to enrich its leaders at the expense of the businesses that fed it, with the result that the "predatory" state drove the economy into an economic decline.

There is much talk today about the need for "good governance". Central elements in how countries are governed are the relationships between state, capital and labour. Many relationships are possible, with the result that some capitalisms are more humane and more productive than others. For example, some major gains for labour have been made in some states and in some periods, especially in the northern European corporatist countries during the period from 1945 to, say, 1990. Outside the core countries, capitalist countries are typically more repressive towards labour, more unequal in their outcomes and less democratic in their polities than their counterparts in the core. As capitalism has evolved in many parts of the world under the aegis of imperialism and colonialism, it has been less amenable to the types of progressive social policies which have been demanded and achieved in many Western capitalist societies. The ability of organized labour to play the same role in developing countries that it has played in most of the core capitalist countries is constrained by its relatively small size (with a large part of the labour force in the agricultural and informal sectors) as well as by the frequency of state repression. The relations between state, capital and labour are rooted in history and while some changes in institutional structures are always possible, and frequently desirable, the scope for such changes is nevertheless constrained by historical factors. Changes in institutional structures do occur, however, as the capitalist revolution in the countries of the former Soviet bloc demonstrate.

The varieties of capitalism are not immune to historical change either. They have been presented here in a static way, designed to highlight their differences. Of course, none of the varieties of capitalism have gone unaltered in the last half of the twentieth century. They have all been faced with pressures for change from domestic and international sources. The next chapter analyses the changes in the nature of capitalism since 1945.

Further reading

For a comprehensive review of the main varieties of capitalism discussed in this chapter, together with an assessment of their relative performances, see David Coates, *Models of Capitalism: Growth and Stagnation in the Modern Era*, Malden, MA: Polity Press, 2000.

The differences between British and Japanese industrial relations systems is discussed in the classic, but now dated, work by Ronald Dore, *British Factory – Japanese Factory: The Origins of National Diversity in Industrial Relations*, Berkeley: University of

California Press, 1973. For an excellent account of capital–labour relations in post-war Japan, see John Price, *Japan Works: Power and Paradox in Postwar Industrial Relations*, Ithaca, NY: ILR/ Cornell University Press, 1991. For the ways in which other countries in East Asia adopted developmentalist institutions and structures, see Gordon White, editor, *Developmental States in East Asia*, London: Macmillan, 1988. For the role of MITI in Japanese economic development, see Chalmers Johnson, *MITI and the Japanese Miracle: The Growth of Industrial Policy 1925–1975*, Stanford, CA: Stanford University Press, 1982.

For differences in welfare state systems, an influential book is Gosta Esping-Andersen's *The Three Worlds of Welfare Capitalism*, Princeton, NJ: Princeton University Press.

The damaging effects of IMF policies on Russia are documented by Joseph Stiglitz, a recent former chief economist at the World Bank, in *Globalization and its Discontents*, London: Norton, 2002. The inequalities arising under Russian capitalism are analysed in Bertram Silverman and Murray Yanowitch, *New Rich, New Poor, New Russia: Winners and Losers on the Russian Road to Capitalism*, second edition, Armonk, NY: Sharpe, 2000. For capitalist models and their applicability to Latin America, see Evelyn Huber, editor, *Models of Capitalism: Lessons for Latin America*, Pennsylvania: The Pennsylvania State Press, 2002.

Notes

1 "Corporatism" is a tricky concept and, like capitalism, can be found in a number of different guises. As well as the consensual form, outlined here, in which the state interacts with independent capital and labour organizations, it can also occur in authoritarian form where the state dominates the other two agents. This "authoritarian

corporatism" has characterized a number of countries in Latin America and East Asia.

2 See Stilwell (2000: Chapter 11) for the Australian case.

3 And, of course, these holders of power have limited the policy choices to alternative models of capitalism. Models based on socialism have often come to an abrupt end, such as in the case of Allende's Chile which resulted in the 1973 military coup. It remains to be seen if new directions arise from the Charez and Morales presidencies in Venezuela and Bolivia respectively.

4 Poverty is defined here as consumption less than one-third of the national average for 1993. See Sheahan (2002: 38).

CHAPTER 6

Post-1945 capitalism: variations over time

Introduction

CAPITALISM IS AN EVER-CHANGING system. The latter half of the twentieth century is no exception. Just as state–capital–labour relations differ between countries, so they vary over time for capitalist countries taken as a whole. Broadly speaking, the latter half of the twentieth century can be divided into three main periods. From 1945 to approximately 1970, the capitalist economies experienced a period of historically rapid growth based on the Bretton Woods agreement which set out the international architecture of the post-war capitalist order and on Keynesianism domestically. This period has been described as a "golden age" in which state, capital and labour combined to produce historically impressive economic results. The policies governing capitalist economies in this period were broadly consistent with those advocated by capitalism's reformist critics outlined in Chapter 3. The 1970s can be seen as a decade of turmoil and crises as firms and states sought to find new ways of restoring profitability in the face of the breakdown of the Bretton Woods order and the failure of Keynesianism to deal effectively with the oil price shocks. The last two decades of the century witnessed the concerted attempt to find "free market" solutions to this profitability crisis, solutions based on giving more power to capital. This is reflected in the ideological ascendancy of what has been called "market fundamentalism" or "neoliberalism": in short, the ascendancy of ideas and policies based on the view that capitalism is a system "natural and free" as outlined in Chapter 2.

1945–70: the "golden age" . . . hot economies, warm capital–labour relations, and the Cold War

At the end of the Second World War, the capitalist countries of Europe which had dominated the globe during the previous three centuries had been severely weakened. The United States now assumed unrivalled leadership of the capitalist bloc. Such was the devastation in Europe that it is estimated that the US accounted for about half of all world industrial output in 1945. The task was to reconstruct capitalist economies and societies in the face of the immediate history of the devastation of two world wars and the Great Depression and the contemporary threat of state socialism, a threat both militarily and ideologically. The historical legacy was addressed through the Bretton Woods agreement. The threat of socialism was also addressed globally – from exposing the communists in Hollywood, to the

Cold War in partitioned Europe and to the support for anti-communist regimes (of varying degrees of unpleasantness) in the decolonizing "Third World".

The task of reconstruction was a tall order. In the 1950s and 1960s, capitalist economies responded by posting their most successful economic results of the century. It was in this period, which economists have sometimes dubbed "the golden age", that generalized living standards increased rapidly in the core capitalist countries. Economic growth was high in a large part of the capitalist developing world, although many of the benefits did not reach the poor. In the core countries, it was in this period that the availability of mass consumer goods expanded and when the spectre of mass unemployment was banished. Certainly economic growth and productivity growth in this period were high by historical standards. It is also true, as Stilwell (2000: 111) notes, "that this may have been a relatively 'golden age' in the economy, with full employment as the norm, but it was also a period when social values were strongly shaped by the politics of the cold war, sexism, racism, and censorship". So, without getting too carried away with nostalgia for the "golden age", it is still important to understand the conditions under which capitalism – of whatever national variety – recovered from a half-century of devastation and instability to perform so well.

The institutional building block of the capitalist system at the international level was the Bretton Woods system (Box 6.1).

Keynesian "demand management" policies were used to smooth the business cycle, with government spending acting as a counter-cyclical stabilizer. That is, when unemployment was increasing, the government would spend more, thereby

BOX 6.1

The Bretton Woods system

This system is named after the conference held at Bretton Woods, New Hampshire, in 1944. It was here that Harry Dexter White, representing the US, and John Maynard Keynes, representing the UK, drew up their blueprint for international post-war stability. This was premised on the belief that the response of the victorious powers to those defeated after the First World War had been punitive and had resulted in social and economic instability. This time, post-war economies and societies were to be reconstructed within an institutional context designed to promote stability. The IBRD (World Bank) was to provide long-term subsidized finance to meet long-term development objectives. A second institution, the IMF, was established to assist countries experiencing short-term balance of payments problems. The Bretton Woods system set up a series of fixed exchange rates with the US dollar as the anchor currency. The US dollar became both a national and an international currency. In order to avoid the competitive devaluations which bedevilled the capitalist economies in the 1930s, exchange rates were to be fixed to the US dollar at rates which would be changed only if it became clear that "economic fundamentals" required some adjustment of these rates. To overcome short-term imbalances, the IMF would provide deficit countries with the liquidity that they required while they undertook the necessary adjustments to their economies. It was the expectation that the burden of adjustment would not fall solely on deficit countries; those running balance of payments surpluses too would be required to make adjustments as well. With external stability organized in this way, internal stability was the responsibility of national governments pursuing the policies required to provide full employment. The Bretton Woods system allowed international trade to expand while at the same time enabling national governments to exercise autonomy in their pursuit of domestic goals.

injecting more demand into the system. If, on the other hand, the economy was running at beyond full employment and inflation was increasing, then the government would run a surplus and reduce the level of demand in the economy. In this way, Keynesianism offered policy-makers the tools with which to provide capitalist economies with the stability which they had so evidently lacked in the inter-war period. In order to enhance national economic policy autonomy, national economies were given some insulation from potentially destabilizing flows of international capital by the use of capital controls. That is, the threat posed to national policies by the flight of capital was significantly lessened by clipping the wings of capital. The stabilization of the capitalist system was premised on giving the state more responsibility and power at the expense of capital, especially of finance capital.

It was in this period too that the welfare state expanded to provide collective insurance against the insecurities of working life under capitalism. In important ways, as indicated in Chapter 3, the welfare state resulted in the, at least partial, "de-commodification" of labour. That is, rewards which individuals received from the economic system no longer depended strictly on their ability to sell their labour on the market. If jobs were not available, through no fault of the individual, then the state would act as the collective insurer and provide individuals with income until jobs were again available. As well as playing this collective insurance role, the state's role expanded as functions such as health and education were taken out of the private sector and made widely available through state provision. As both a means of increasing the productivity of the national economy and a means of ensuring that the benefits of economic growth were more equally shared, the state's role in the provision of health and education expanded.

The result of these policies was that in the 1950s and 1960s capitalist countries in the core grew at historically unprecedented rates, secured levels of employment which had never previously been achieved for such a long period and had institutional mechanisms in place, such as the welfare state and progressive taxation, which ensured that income inequality generally decreased over the period. This combination of investment by capital based on an expanding mass market, full employment for labour with expanding welfare state services and restrained wage demands, and an interventionist role for the state has often been described as constituting a "capital–labour accord", a "capital–labour compromise", a "capital–labour settlement" or a "post-war settlement". This was most obviously the case in the European corporatist countries but it was also evident in the other varieties of capitalism. How long this settlement could last is a matter of conjecture; by the end of the 1960s there were already evident tensions between capital and labour.

In any event, while the internal economic stability of capitalist economies in the core achieved by this "settlement" provided for a "golden age", the political instability of the global face-off between capitalism and state socialism was taking its toll, not only in human lives but also in the ability of the system to continue unchanged. While living standards rose impressively in the capitalist West, they also did so in the Soviet Union during this period. Unlikely as it may seem now, the question then was not if, but when, the Soviet Union would catch up with the US as an economic power. Stalin's forced industrialization path, purchased at high human cost, seemed to be capable of matching the West economically. The fact that the Soviet Union won the race to put the first person in space seemed to confirm this. And the state socialist system was attracting new converts.

After the nineteenth century had seen the uninterrupted (although not unchallenged or peaceful) expansion of the geographical reach of capitalism as more and more countries were integrated into empires and trading relations, the twentieth century saw an increasing diminution of its geographical scope. The Russian revolution in 1917 was followed by the establishment of the Soviet satellites in Eastern Europe as a result of the 1945 Yalta conference. Mao's victory in China in 1949 and Castro's in Cuba a decade later saw state socialist regimes established there. Later, African countries such as Angola, Ethiopia, Yemen and Mozambique would be added to the list.

In Asia, following the stalemate in Northeast Asia in Korea in the early 1950s, the US was in no mood to let Vietnam go the same way and Southeast Asia became the new battleground. The Vietnam War, in addition to its human cost, seriously compromised the ability of the US dollar to act as both a national currency and the international anchor currency. In the end, the economic strains imposed by the war led to these dual roles being incompatible, and the US was forced to make the dollar inconvertible against gold and to depreciate its value. The Bretton Woods system was effectively over and the 1970s were to confront capitalist countries with a new set of problems – and instabilities.

Before coming to these, a few words are necessary on capitalism outside the core, in the Third World, in those developing countries which remained in the capitalist camp by popular choice or by the support given by the West (especially the US) to anti-communist dictators.

The "golden age" in the South: post-colonial capitalist states seek modernity and industrialization

Developing countries shared in the growth of the post-1945 international economy, although mainly on the basis of the export of primary commodities. Along with the expansion of world trade, international transfers in the form of foreign aid also increased. Politically, aid served the purpose of providing an incentive for developing countries to stay within the capitalist camp and tied their interests to those of the donors. Economically, aid was regarded as necessary to kick-start their economies so that they too could pursue the path to capitalist riches. Walter Rostow's (1960) influential book, *The Stages of Economic Growth*, pointedly subtitled *A Non-Communist Manifesto*, provided the arguments. Countries, he argued, all went through the same stages. The key for developing countries was to break out of their "traditional" stage and embark on the process of "modernization", a process requiring a sufficiently high investable surplus to permit growth to take place. Also required was the replacement of "traditional" with "modern" institutions and ways of thinking – that is, institutions and ways of thinking favourable to market expansion and capitalist accumulation. In this, Rostow was following the well-worn path of arguing that the "enabling environment" for capitalism needed to be created just as it had been in seventeenth- and eighteenth-century Europe (and, subsequently, in 1990s' Russia). Foreign aid could help supplement investment funds so that the stage of "take-off" could be reached. "Modern" cultures and institutions could be stimulated by allowing foreign firms to operate and thereby

"transfer technology", and by removing social and cultural constraints to the "spirit of capitalism". The "market" needed to be
unleashed so that it could play the same ("spontaneous") role
that it had done in the core countries.

Not all developing countries were convinced of the wisdom of
this free-market approach which seemed to limit national aspirations by confining them to be producers of primary commodities
for the industrialized West. This resembled the colonial trade,
which fitted uneasily with post-colonial aspirations. Developing
countries which had rejected the Soviet state socialist path to
industrialization were nevertheless unimpressed by free-trade
doctrines. Instead a significant number of them, especially in
Latin America and East Asia, attempted to overcome their
"dependant" status by an industrialization strategy which
involved substantial state intervention in the economy. This
became associated with the "import substitution" industrialization strategy, pioneered by the UN's Economic Commission
for Latin America, whereby countries sought to produce domestically the manufactured goods which they currently imported.
To assist in this process, high tariff barriers were put in place to
prevent competition from imports. Thus, in Brazil, for example,
automobile manufacturing started in this way. The firms producing for this domestic developing country market were typically
multinational corporations, which, deterred by selling directly by
high tariffs, set up production behind the tariff walls. Developing
countries, in return, sought to regulate the activities of the
multinationals by stipulating, for example, how much they
had to purchase from local suppliers and how much profit they
could repatriate. Capitalist development was again seen as a
national project in which states regulated capital in the "national

interest". Of course, the interests of some were better served than others in this process.

In general, the developing countries' economies grew at sustained and high rates during the 1950s and, somewhat less impressively, during the 1960s. Many social indicators such as life expectancy and child mortality also showed dramatic improvement. However, politically, many were under the grips of nationalist authoritarian regimes, often kept in power by Western backers. Nationalism and nation-building often provided a framework for the suppression of labour and minority rights. The agenda of developing countries – to use their post-colonial political independence to increase their economic independence through industrialization – was only partly successful. This led to calls in the 1970s by developing countries for the establishment of a New International Economic Order. Central to this order were a commitment to a fairer distribution of world income to be achieved through mechanisms such as increased foreign aid, controls over multinationals to ensure that there was a transfer of technology, and the stabilization of volatile international commodity prices. Even in the "golden age" of capitalism, world income inequality appeared as a constant concern and focus for discontent.

The 1970s: oil shocks the system . . . and Keynesian policy responses

The countries in the capitalist core were soon to be too concerned about the disruption to their own economic order to worry too much about the demands of developing countries. The breakdown of the Bretton Woods system came just as the international economy was faced with its biggest economic shock since 1945 in the form of the tripling of the price of oil in 1973. The Organization of Petroleum Exporting Countries (OPEC) used its market power to raise the price of oil and to keep the price there by agreements among its members to restrict output. This resulted in a huge increase in the flow of resources to the various Middle Eastern sheikdoms and authoritarianisms which produced the vast majority of the world's oil at the time. The industrialized countries of the capitalist core responded to the 1973 oil price shock by attempting to restrict short-term oil consumption through mechanisms such as rationing, bans on Sunday driving, and lower speed limits. Medium-term measures were introduced, such as increasing the supply of oil from other sources (such as the North Sea), switching to the use of other power sources (nuclear, coal and natural gas) and encouraging greater fuel efficiency, especially for automobiles.

In terms of economic policy, the response by core capitalist states was generally to try to maintain levels of employment and to run balance of payments deficits rather than engage in draconian cuts in spending. However, the outcome was "stagflation" – a combination of a stagnating economy and high inflation. The Keynesian demand management policies which had been so successful in fine-tuning economies in the 1950s and 1960s were premised on the assumption that economies would be faced with either inflation or unemployment. Now, the core capitalist economies were increasingly threatened with both, with the result that Keynesian-style policies were cast into serious doubt. Capital–labour tensions rose across the core capitalist countries, although the more consensual corporatist countries were better able to contain them. In the absence of the two pillars of the post-1945 "golden age", namely, the Bretton Woods international order and Keynesian policies domestically, capitalist states' responses through the 1970s became increasingly bereft of ideas. A general "muddling through" pragmatism proved unable to restore growth and profitability.

A new international division of labour: the lure of cheap labour in the South

Large firms began to significantly shift manufacturing production overseas. The crisis of profitability led multinational firms to expand their sphere of production in the search for lower labour costs. Developing countries had long been integrated into the international capitalist economy on the basis of supplying the raw materials for industrial country production, as we saw in Chapter 4. The mining, oil and agribusiness multinationals were the major players in these markets. Developing country markets too were opened up to the manufactured goods of core countries. In the 1960s, as noted, production by manufacturing multinationals in and for developing country markets was encouraged by the high tariff policies used by developing countries at the time.

Now, however, a *new* international division of labour was created in which developing countries became the source of low-cost labour for manufacturing firms selling their products primarily in the core country markets. Everything from clothing to electronics shifted to developing country production sites in response to lower labour costs. The flip side of this was a process of "de-industrialization" in the core countries as many "traditional" industries disappeared from their geographical and economic landscapes.

The 1980s and 1990s: the rise of neoliberalism ... capital strikes back

Over the course of these two decades there would be a complete reformulation of the ways of governing capitalist economies. The elections of Reagan and Thatcher, following the morass of economic policy in the 1970s and aggravated by a further oil price increase in 1979, ushered in an era of unprecedented ideological assault on the central tenets of post-1945 economic management and social policy at both the domestic and international levels. The "post-1945 settlement" which characterized the "golden age" involved a greater role for the state in the economy and an acceptance of its responsibility for full employment and social equity. This was the case in the Anglo-American version of capitalism and even more obviously the case in the northern European corporatist countries. The market fundamentalist or neoliberal revolution of the 1980s, spearheaded in the Anglo-American world, sought to tear up the settlement. The state was reconceptualized as less interventionist and less responsible for economic outcomes. Labour was weakened both by reducing the power of trade unions and by eliminating the "generosity" of the welfare state. Capital was freed from its regulatory constraints. The "Keynesian moment" had lasted for more than two decades but it was now decisively over. In terms of the discussion in Chapter 3, the capitalist state acted as it needed to do in order to create the conditions intended to restore profitability and the continued viability of the capitalist system.

The basic tenets of "neoliberal" ideology and policies (Box 6.2) will be familiar to most, especially those who have lived in the UK or the US since the 1980s, although their influence is

BOX 6.2

Neoliberalism

Neoliberalism describes the view that markets are the best
way of organizing production and that state intervention is to be
generally minimized. For this reason, neoliberalism is sometimes
also referred to as "market fundamentalism". It is based on the
premise that capitalism works best when capitalists are able to
operate with only limited restrictions placed upon them. This is
exactly what was argued by capitalism's supporters as surveyed
in Chapter 2. Adam Smith was an economic liberal; the return to
ascendancy of views similar to his today marks a *neo*liberalism.
The prefix "neo", meaning new, has more to do with the new
context and new time within which the policies associated with
neoliberalism (free trade and privatization, for example) are being
introduced than anything particularly new about the views and
policies which it represents. The term "neoliberalism" is used
widely today, especially among its critics. It can be thought of as
shorthand for the arguments for capitalism as a system which is
"natural" and "free".

clearly evident elsewhere. What may be unfamiliar to younger
readers is the extent to which these ideas and policies were
once highly controversial and had to fight for dominance. Their
ascendancy has become so widespread that it is difficult to grasp
now that there was a time when they were not.

Attack inflation. Don't worry about unemployment . . .

One of the major changes which occurred in this period was
the repudiation of the state's responsibility to provide full

employment. In the UK this responsibility was enshrined in the post-war Beveridge Report but by the 1980s its vision of the state's responsibility was under sustained assault. Part of the assault was waged by the rehabilitation of "monetarism", and in particular the theories of Milton Friedman, as a theory of economic management in the UK under Thatcher and, a little later, by "supply side economics" in the US under Reagan. While there are some important differences between the two at the level of theory, the policy implications were broadly overlapping in terms of their common desires to reduce the size of the state sector in the economy, allow capital to operate more freely, and reduce other impediments to market "flexibility". Since monetarism is now largely discredited as a theory of economic management and is not the official policy of any of the core capitalist states, it is difficult to imagine now the credence given to its high priests in the 1980s. Under their influence, the key concern of the government became inflation, with full employment being downgraded and then disappearing as an explicit state responsibility. This shift in economic policy focus was gradually accepted in just about all of the core capitalist countries.

. . . or the unemployed . . .

Unemployment became to be – or rather reverted to being – regarded as more of a personal failing than a failure of the capitalist system. Individuals were either not skilled enough, had the wrong skills, or were insufficiently enterprising in their search for work. As the monetarist experiment caused a recession which sent interest rates and unemployment sharply upwards, and greatly increased the numbers of long-term unemployed (i.e.

those unemployed for more than a year), the ideological battle turned to portraying these consequences not as policy failures but as individual failings and as an unfortunate but necessary part of the process of "short-term pain for long-term gain". In short, many of the arguments used in the 1930s returned.

With unemployment viewed in this way, the agenda was opened for a redefining of the welfare state. Its success in "de-commodifying labour", that is, in removing from labour the absolute necessity of market participation, was seen as problematic and as being too beneficial for individuals. There has been a general move towards the resurrection of Victorian distinctions of the "deserving and undeserving poor" with the object of policy being to reduce the generosity of the system to the (ever-expanding) latter category. Conditions of eligibility for welfare state payments have been continually tightened and the value and length of unemployment benefits reduced. In general, to use Thatcher's words, the welfare state was re-theorized as the "nanny state", clearly not one appropriate for "free" individuals.

The view of the welfare state as an agency for collective insurance against the vagaries of capitalist instability and as an agent for social mobility was repudiated. In its place the welfare state was increasingly portrayed as a stifler of individual initiative, a form of unwelcome "dependency" on the state, a disincentive to greater geographical mobility, and a site of bureaucracy and economic inefficiency which needed to operate on market lines. In short, the welfare state was the enemy of the "enterprise culture" which the neoliberal revolution sought to promote to solve capitalism's problems.

This, of course, also had implications for gender relations. As explained in Chapter 5, the Anglo-American version of the welfare state envisaged a "dual breadwinner, female carer" gender contract. With the rise of family breakdowns and the increase in single-parent (predominantly female-headed) households, this contract was obviously in need of revision. In its meanest form, this has led to the emergence of a "single breadwinner, single carer" model in which single mothers are required to work in order to be eligible to continue to receive other forms of welfare payments but are still responsible for the care of their children. The child's age at which the requirement for single mothers to work starts has been progressively reduced. While this policy of requiring single mothers to leave their children and to work (often for minimum wages), a policy common throughout much of North America, can only be described as mean and counter-productive, its widespread implementation shows the power of the ideological message that single mothers need to be "rescued from welfare dependency".

. . . make those employed more "flexible" . . .

The refashioning of the welfare state was also justified by the need to encourage labour market "flexibility". The need for such flexibility arose in part, it was argued, because of the demands of the technological revolution under way and was usually associated with the information, computer and telecommunications industries. This revolution has transformed the ways in which industries operate, with the ability to send information around the globe at minimal cost being but one example. In this new information age, workers need to be capable of performing multiple tasks and firms need to be able to rely on permanent workers but also to be able to contract out employment where necessary. The shift towards "post-Fordist" production methods required flexible labour markets. To the extent that welfare states reduced flexibility, then they too needed to be reformed.

The whole thrust of labour market "deregulation" was to make labour markets more responsive to changing industry needs. What was at stake here, though, was not simply an issue of responsiveness but the reshaping of the power relations between capital and labour in the workplace. "Deregulation" usually involved removing some forms of protection for workers and giving employers more power to change the timing and conditions of work. Labour market deregulation placed additional strains on women performing the dual functions of breadwinner and carer, whether in one- or two-parent households. Trade unions were directly targeted for reduced power. This came about through changing the legislation which governed their activities, from election and strike procedures to the closed shop and secondary picketing in the UK, to the support for union-free states in the US. The defeat of the year-long miners' strike in the UK in the early 1980s also marked a turning point in the power of organized labour, a group that Thatcher had termed "the enemy within".

. . . and remove restrictions on capital

At the same time as labour was being restricted in these ways, capital was being freed of many of the regulatory constraints of the state. This was most obviously the case for finance capital. In the post-1945 period, capital controls were considered a normal part of the economic armoury of states wishing to pursue national objectives such as full employment. Financial markets were subject to the control of nation states. In the neoliberal agenda, financial markets were seen as important mechanisms for ensuring that investment funds were allocated to the most profitable projects; state regulations which hampered the flow of financial resources were therefore sources of inefficiency. States embarked on a policy of financial market liberalization (witness London's and Tokyo's "Big Bangs") which enabled finance capital (in the form of equity funds, for example) to search the globe for the highest returns. The same opportunities were offered to multinational companies as I will discuss shortly.

Another way in which the opportunities for capital were increased was through a systematic policy of opening up new markets to private businesses. This was not simply a question of geographical scope but also of removing activities from the public sphere back into the private sphere. This policy – now widely known as privatization – sought to restore to private business key areas of economic activity, from telecommunications to transport to energy. These privatizations were carried out throughout many parts of the capitalist core, although again most enthusiastically in the Anglo-American part. The sale of public (or nationalized) industries was relatively easily and quickly accomplished. More recent attempts to extend the example into education and, especially, healthcare have met with more protracted resistance from citizens unwilling to put back into the market sphere that which has been operated according to a different set of principles and priorities over the past half-century. Continuing debates over "public–private partnerships" in many countries indicate that this issue is far from settled.

To further support the restoration of capital's dominance in the economy, neoliberalism's supporters also argued that in order to flourish, the "culture of enterprise" needed the state not only to remove direct regulations on its activities but also to stop penalizing, through taxation, its successes. Rates of taxation on high income earners and "risk-taking" investors were greatly reduced. In the US the tax reductions given to the rich reached obscene proportions during the 1980s and 1990s, with each new President seemingly intent on outdoing his predecessor in extending tax "relief" to the rich. The result of labour market deregulation on the one hand, which removed from low-paid workers some basic protections, and tax cuts for the rich on the other, resulted in a reversal of inequality trends. After two decades of falling income inequality across the capitalist core, in the 1980s and 1990s income inequality increased again in many countries. As MIT economist Lester Thurow (1996: 21) explains in the case of the US, "in the decade of the 1980s, all the gains in male earnings went to the top 20 percent of the workforce and an amazing 64 percent accrued to the top 1 percent". And while inequality increased, a large part of the workforce was faced with falling real wages (i.e. wages adjusted for what they can purchase). Again, as Thurow (1996: 24) explains, "from 1973 to 1994, America's real per capita GNP rose 33 percent, yet real hourly wages fell 14 percent and real weekly wages 19 percent for nonsupervisory workers (those males and females who do not boss anyone else). By the end of 1994 real wages were back to where they had been in the late 1950s."

While many large corporations escaped the inconvenience of paying taxation altogether, food banks became a permanent feature of advanced capitalist societies (especially in North America, despite its large agricultural surpluses) and homeless-ness spread from the US to all of the major cities of the capitalist core as the holes in welfare state safety nets became increasingly large.[1] And now, in the first decade of the new century, the pressures are for "flat taxes" based on the view that the rich should pay no greater proportion of their income to the state than the poor. Then, everyone will be treated "equally" and enterprise will not be punished; Hayek's view of "just" taxation will have prevailed.

The rise of neoliberalism, therefore, was premised on the need to find a way out of the impasse of the stagflation and the rising tensions between capital and labour which threatened profitability across the core capitalist economies in the 1970s. The resulting move to strengthen capital, weaken labour and reduce the direct role of the state in the economy (although maintaining its critical disciplining role) indicated the nature of the neoliberal response. The faith in the market as a method of economic coordination was accompanied by an ideological assault on the main tenets of the Keynesian-inspired post-1945 settlement which underpinned the "golden age". This assault included a rejection of the state as a vehicle for progressive social transformation and a stress on the need to increase the "liberty" of the individual against the incursions of the state. Such liberty was to be realized through the market.

The ideological case for neoliberalism was critical to its ascendancy because its economic results were unimpressive. Of course, some did get rich, most notably those who were already rich. Fortunes were made on stock markets and in real estate. The high-tech sector temporarily boomed. Media barons rejoiced as they expanded their empires. Bank profits continued their inexorable rise. The rest were left to deal with increasing inequality, increasing economic insecurity and growth rates that remained much below their "golden age" levels. The ideological case was much more successful, therefore, than its associated economic policies. In addition, there was a systematic attempt to fashion a "popular capitalism" in which a "property-owning democracy", i.e. one in which voters all had economic interests in the maintenance of the capitalist system, was promoted through the sale of public housing at great discount in the UK and through mass privatizations and preferential share purchases here and elsewhere. But perhaps the most important factor was the constant explicit and implicit appeal to "trickle down" economics, that is, the argument that the interests of the rich and the poor are strongly interdependent. It is the rich who employ the poor and so without the prosperity of the former, the lot of the latter would be even worse. This also represents a return to Victorian thinking with its implied stress on hierarchy and deference.

The ideological pre-eminence of neoliberalism and its policy revolution were, as already noted, followed most clearly in the Anglo-American cases. However, the ramifications were felt world-wide and many of the policies outlined above were followed, at least in part, in many countries. This compromised the other varieties of capitalism which were described in the last chapter. For example, as David Coates (2000: 100) argues, the removal of capital controls in Sweden in 1985 led to a large export of capital by Swedish firms. The result was a sharp reduction in "the willingness of Swedish capital to tolerate the costs and constraints imposed upon it hitherto by the power of Swedish labour" (2000: 100–101). In the 1990s, the Swedish model was in crisis in no small part because of the increased power obtained by capital in the wake of "globalization". Thurow (1996: 5) is more blunt in arguing that "while the social welfare state [i.e. the northern European corporatist model] did not collapse, it has essentially gone broke". Blairite visions of a "Third Way" accept the ideological premises of neoliberalism and only tinker with its details; it is, in former Labour deputy leader Roy Hattersley's apt description, no more than "benevolent Thatcherism".[2] For Wolfgang Streeck (2001: 38), the changes brought by neoliberalism "would seem to amount not just to another wave of economic liberalization, but to a perhaps permanent dismantling of collective capacity to resist liberalization", a dismantling which has already significantly reduced the non-liberal (or interventionist) character of German and Japanese capitalism. These issues will be discussed further in the next chapter, but before leaving the topic here, it is important to note that the changes in economic ideology and policy after 1980 were felt fully in developing countries as well.

Neoliberalism in the South: open those doors, be "market friendly"!

The rise of neoliberalism in the core countries was matched by the changing intellectual attitudes of the World Bank and the IMF and was reflected in their shift to "conditionality" lending as a response to the international debt crisis of the early 1980s.[3] The onset of monetarism in the core countries drove interest rates up and induced a recession which slowed developing country exports. For the developing countries this meant that their debt payments went up just as their ability to earn the foreign exchange to pay them went down; the result was an international debt crisis in which many countries faced the prospect of default without more borrowing from the IMF. The latter was therefore called upon but made its lending conditional on economic reforms in the borrowing countries. These conditions, embodied in IMF stabilization policies and World Bank structural adjustment packages (Box 6.3), were drawn from the neoliberal textbook.

BOX 6.3

Structural adjustment programmes

These are programmes which developing countries must implement in return for receiving loans from the IMF and World Bank. Although they are designed to address the problems of individual countries, they are based on a common set of "reforms". Applied to dozens of countries in all regions of the world outside the capitalist core, the standard reforms included reducing the size of government, opening borders to trade and foreign investment, privatization and encouraging integration into the global economy. This often means removing price subsidies on food and energy, reducing public expenditure, removing import controls and eliminating restrictions on foreign firms. When introduced, the reforms have often provoked popular riots. Critics argue that the effect of the programmes has been to increase poverty.

The use of structural adjustment programmes, introduced in the early 1980s and used widely since, represents the imposition of neoliberal economic policies on developing countries. This neoliberalism was embraced with some enthusiasm by ruling elites in many Latin American countries and in some transition economies in the former Soviet bloc, was begrudgingly accepted in many Southeast Asian countries (although not without some resistance) and was imposed amid institutional collapse in many sub-Saharan African countries.

This change in development strategy required both finance and technology; in short, it required the rehabilitation of the multinational corporation. As part of the new "market friendly" approach to development advocated by the World Bank, requirements placed upon multinationals were reduced as developing countries sought to attract increasing amounts of scarce global foreign direct investment to their shores. From the Caribbean to Mauritius to China, multinationals were courted as the harbingers of development. And just as developing countries were courting foreign direct investment, multinationals themselves were searching for lower-cost production sites. Developing countries turned to what has been variously termed "export-led growth", "foreign direct investment-led growth" or, because of the labour force employed in many of the manufacturing zones around the world, "female-led growth". Flushed with this embrace of foreign private capital, developing countries also began liberalizing capital accounts, allowing free currency convertibility and opening "emerging" bond and equity markets to foreign purchasers. The new international division of labour based on the production of labour-intensive manufactures in developing countries can be dated from the mid-1970s as a response to the profitability crisis in industrial countries. However, the largest increases in private capital flows were not to come for another decade.

By the mid-1980s the building blocks were in place for an explosion in international financial flows: deregulation of financial markets in the US and UK under the ideology of neoliberalism, a search by multinationals for cheaper production sites overseas, and market-opening by many developing countries. Added to this, in the period 1989–91 another 400 million people were brought into the ambit of global capitalism as state socialism collapsed in Russia and Eastern Europe. The result was a dramatic increase in global capital flows. And with the greater flows came greater financial turmoil.

Global turbulence: financial crises in the 1990s

The 1990s witnessed a spate of financial crises throughout the world and ushered in a decade of what has been termed "global turbulence". The Japanese stock market "bubble" of the late 1980s burst and the stock market fell precipitously; the Nikkei Index was no higher in 2006 than it was in 1986 and Japan has been stuck in a protracted and seemingly unsolvable recession since 1990. In 1992, the European exchange rate mechanism fell apart after speculators believed that existing exchange rates could no longer be sustained. Britain and Italy were forced to leave the system. Sweden increased short-term interest rates to 500 percent to try, in vain, to protect its currency. In 1994, Mexico became the next case. Mexico had turned to neoliberalism as the solution to its economic ills in the late 1980s and had introduced a programme of rapid trade liberalization, privatization and deregulation. International investors liked what they saw and capital flowed into the country. Entry into NAFTA on 1 January 1994 cemented these policy reforms. Quite unexpectedly, however, by the end of that year Mexico found itself embroiled in a currency crisis which saw the peso devalued by 50 percent, GDP fall by 6 per cent and the financial system left in ruins.

In 1997–98 it was Asia's turn. Starting in Thailand in July 1997, currencies throughout the region came under attack by speculators who felt that devaluations were inevitable and did not want to be caught as the last person holding a devalued currency. Financial crises swept the region, with country after country – with the notable exception of Malaysia – turning to the IMF for assistance. By the time the dust had settled, the IMF had instituted the largest bailout in its history with a US$54 billion loan to South Korea. Indonesia received US$40 billion, Thailand US$17.2 billion and the Philippines US$1 billion. To many observers, including former World Bank chief economist Joseph Stiglitz, the IMF conditions attached to its "rescue package" made the situation in these countries even worse. The application of standard neoliberal principles – cutting government spending, opening up the economy further to foreign investment – drove the economies further into recession. Then came further crises in Russia and Brazil in 1998 and in Argentina in 2001. Suddenly, the 1990s looked like the 1870s (reviewed in Chapter 4) with their constant financial crises.

"Crony capitalism" blamed for the Asian crises

In analysing these financial crises, many neoliberal commentators pointed not to the endemic speculation in financial markets as the cause of global turbulence but to the policies of the crisis-affected countries themselves. For example, in the Asian case, the blame was placed on the form of capitalism which prevailed in the region and which was subsequently dubbed "crony capitalism". The problem was, the argument went, that governments and businesses were too close in their relationships and, as a result, businesses borrowed too much and invested too riskily on the assumption that their friends in the government would bail them out if they erred; in short, if successful the business would reap the private profit, and if unsuccessful the government would pay the public cost.

For some, therefore, the financial crisis pointed to the end of the "Asian developmental model" (outlined in the last chapter) and the triumph of what then Federal Reserve Chairman Alan Greenspan called "Market Capitalism" (or the Anglo-American model). According to Greenspan's (1998) analysis, "the [Asian] crises have their roots in the endeavor of some East Asian countries to open up their economies to world competition, while still mandating a significant proportion of their output through government directives. . . . Partial planning of the sort practiced by some East Asian countries can look very successful for a time . . . But there are limits to this process as economies mature . . . Eventually and inevitably, however, such a regime leads to establish facilities that produce goods and services that domestic consumers and export customers apparently no longer want. . . . [A]s a consequence of the experience of the last half century, market capitalism has clearly become ascendant, at least for now."

Remove the plank from your own eye, Mr Greenspan!

One suspects that Alan Greenspan's temporal qualifier "at least for now" was intended to last more than the three years between his assessment of the failings of East Asian capitalism and the collapse of US company Enron amid a scandal that rocked the foundations of "market capitalism" in late 2001. The "crony capitalism" of East Asian developmental capitalism appeared in a new guise in US-style market capitalism. Only here, it was not the government and businesses that were too close but businesses and their auditors. After initiating a report to unravel the tangled web of corporate practice surrounding Enron, US Senate

Finance Committee Chair Charles Grassley said "The report reads like a conspiracy novel, with some of the nation's finest banks, accounting firms and attorneys working together to prop up the biggest corporate farce of this century."[4] The world's largest bankruptcy, that of WorldCom, followed shortly after the Enron collapse, again amid accusations of corporate wrongdoings. More has followed as Wall Street's leading investment firms were found guilty of deliberately being overly optimistic about stocks in order to boost their business; under "popular capitalism" small investors were easy prey for the corporate sharks.[5] The unbridled market capitalism ushered in by neoliberalism since the 1980s revealed that capitalism could not be trusted to regulate itself.

Fin-de-siècle complexities

The post-1945 period started with capitalism facing the challenge of its past and being confronted with a shrinking geographical space as state socialism spread across parts of the world. The institutional frameworks put in place internationally and domestically resulted in a remarkable two-decade "golden age". The frameworks unravelled in the 1970s and the solution proposed from the 1980s onwards was a "market fundamentalist" or "neoliberal" framework which reduced the role of the state, gave priority to "the market", reduced the power of labour and increased that of capital. The economic results did not match those of the "golden age" but an ideological ascendancy had been established. With this came financial crises and a decade of "global turbulence" as capitalist instability returned with a vengeance.

At the beginning of the millennium, capitalism stands in a new but complex position. There are echoes of the past as the ideological ascendancy of neoliberalism recalls nineteenth-century views of the benefits of the unconstrained role of the market together with a Victorian "blame the victim" moralism masquerading as social policy. In other ways, the twentieth century seems distant, as the challenger to capitalism throughout much of that century, state socialism, has collapsed, leaving capitalism dominant over the whole globe. In still other ways, the information, communications and technological revolution has brought entirely new ways of linking production together across this capitalist globe and points to a technologically distinct twenty-first century. This complex "global capitalism" is the subject of the final chapter.

Further reading

The operation of the Bretton Woods system is covered in many introductory books on post-1945 economic history. A more specialized treatment is given in Peter Kenen, *The International Economy*, Cambridge: Cambridge University Press, 2000. The "golden age" in the core capitalist countries is discussed in Stephen Marglin and Juliet Schor's edited collection, *The Golden Age of Capitalism: Reinterpreting the Postwar Experience*, Oxford: Clarendon Press, 1990. Surendra Patel's "In tribute to the golden age of the South's development", *World Development*, May 1992 (vol. 20, no. 5, pp. 767–771) argues for such an age in the South as well, although he extends the time frame for this age up to 1980 and even, in some respects, up to 1990. The details of the calls for a New International Economic Order are analysed by a range of authors in Jagdish Bhagwati's edited volume, *The New International Economic Order and the North–South Debate*, Cambridge, MA: MIT Press, 1977.

For an analysis of the ways in which states removed the regulations on capital as a result of the rise of neoliberalism, see Eric Helleiner's insightful book, *States and the Reemergence of Global Finance: From Bretton Woods to the 1990s*, Ithaca, NY: Cornell University Press, 1994. For a discussion of the accompanying changes in labour markets and the rise of "labour market flexibility", see Jamie Peck, *Work-Place: The Social Regulation of Labor Markets*, New York: Guilford Press, 1996. The economic results of the neoliberal period are compared with those of the "golden age" in David Coates, *Models of Capitalism: Growth and Stagnation in the Modern Era*, Malden, MA: Polity Press, 2000.

The prescription that developing countries should adopt "market friendly" policies is set out in the World Bank's *World Development Report 1991*, Oxford: Oxford University Press. The ways in which theorizing about development in the South has changed over the post-war period are explained well in Colin Leys's *The Rise and Fall of Development Theory*, Bloomington, IN: Indiana University Press, 1996. The effects of IMF and World Bank policies, through structural adjustment programmes, have been analysed by many authors. For a critical view see Michel Chossudovsky, *The Globalization of Poverty: The Impact of IMF and World Bank Reforms*, London: Zed Press, 1997.

For an overview of the Asian crisis, and of the competing explanations for it, see Brian MacLean, Paul Bowles and Osvaldo Croci, "East Asian crises and regional economic integration", in A. Rugman and G. Boyd (editors), *Deepening Integration in the Pacific Economies: Corporate Alliances, Contestable Markets and Free*

Trade, Cheltenham: Edward Elgar, 1999. See also Joseph Stiglitz, *Globalization and its Discontents*, London: Norton, 2002. For a discussion of various policies designed to prevent repeats of the 1990s financial crises, see Barry Eichengreen's *Financial Crises and What To Do About Them*, Oxford: Oxford University Press, 2002.

There has been a spate of books published in the wake of various corporate collapses and scandals. Two worth reading are Peter Fusaro and Ross Miller, *What Went Wrong at Enron*, New York: Wiley, 2002 and Lynne Jeter, *Disconnected: Deceit and Betrayal at WorldCom*, New York: Wiley, 2003.

Notes

1 According to Thurow (1996: 29), "homelessness began in the United States in the late 1970s. Initially the rest of the industrial world saw 'homelessness' as a phenomenon peculiar to an inadequate American social safety net, but homelessness has now spread throughout the industrial world."

2 Roy Hattersley, "I'm Blair's biggest critic – but he must not quit now", *The Observer*, 11 January 2004, Internet edition.

3 The following three paragraphs draw on Bowles (2000).

4 As quoted in David Teather, "Scandal of crashed company's tax evasion", *The Guardian*, 14 February 2003, Internet edition.

5 See David Usborne, "Shamed Wall Street takes its punishment", *The Independent*, 29 April 2003, Internet edition.

CHAPTER 7

Global capitalism[1]

All the world's a stage . . .

CAPITALISM'S REACH HAS BECOME GLOBAL (again). Many developing countries have become more integrated into the global economy as a result of their liberalization policies. This includes China which has dramatically "opened up" its economy since 1978 and which is now among the world's largest recipients of foreign direct investment flows. The Soviet bloc collapsed at the end of the 1980s. We have entered a new period of "globalization". All the world has become a capitalist stage.

"Global issues" have emerged everywhere. Environmental problems such as global warming have highlighted the interdependencies between countries. The language of human rights has been globalized so that countries are increasingly held to account to universal norms, with the establishment of the International Court of Criminal Justice a reflection of this. Health problems have become global, with the spread of HIV/AIDS and SARs providing examples of how viruses are no respecters of national borders. So too the borders of nation states have become more porous to the flow of drugs, to money laundering and financial crime, and to terrorism. Health, justice and the environment are no longer exclusively national concerns but have become increasingly globalized issues.

The global reach of goods and services means that it is possible to travel the world staying in identical hotels, eating in identical restaurants, consuming identical soft drinks and wearing identical fashion wear, so that the illusion can be created that the traveller has never left "home". The global dominance of brand names and the promotion of homogeneous wants through advertising have created a global consumer culture.

Important economic institutions, and the protests against their policies, are now increasingly global. Annual meetings of international bodies such as the IMF and the World Bank as well as of the G-8 heads of state attract "anti-globalization" protests. The meetings of the world's business leaders and politicians at the World Economic Summit in Davos are countered by meetings of "anti-globalizers" at the World Social Forum. Opposition to the war in Iraq was organized through "global marches".

While all of these trends are evident, and "globalization" may appear obvious, interpreting these trends is a highly contested area. For this reason, authors offer us an "understanding" of, the "capturing" of, and even the "truth" about, the "enigma" of "globalization".[2]

To see why interpreting "globalization" is controversial, the "naming" problem must again be confronted. "Globalization", to use the most widespread term, is simply a pseudonym for global capitalism. The questions that must be asked are how, and to what extent, does contemporary capitalism – global capitalism –

represent a new phase of capitalism? Is it new at all? If so, in what ways? And what are the implications?

Four main answers can be found to these questions. They are distinguished here on the basis of their view of the relationship between "states" and "markets". The concept of the "market" is problematic because it is a term which hides what is really important, namely, the identity of the actors in that market. "Markets" do not exist independently of human action but are, of course, mechanisms through which humans interact. "Markets", therefore, refer to the interactions of individuals and human organizations. Under capitalism, the markets are populated by private firms and, in the labour market, by workers.

. . . but only capital is free to move across it

When it comes to the debates over globalization, the labour market as a global market is, in general, of little importance. Certainly, the global sex trade, Internet brides and migrating workers are significant and, in some cases, very significant. There is also an illegal trade in "people smuggling". But, in many ways, labour is less globally mobile at the start of the twenty-first century than it has been at most other points during the past two centuries; certainly the mass migrations of the nineteenth century have no contemporary parallel. In fact the markets for labour remain predominantly national markets. If workers, particularly low-skilled workers from developing countries, seek to increase their earnings by migrating to richer countries, they are usually denounced as "economic migrants" and sent packing. However, if firms, particularly large firms from core countries, seek to increase their earnings by migrating to lower-cost countries, they are usually welcomed with open arms as "foreign investors". Thus, when we talk about the power of "the market" *vis-à-vis* the state in the context of contemporary globalization, we are really talking about the power of private firms and their ability to act subject to increasingly fewer controls by national governments; this is the context for the debate over the extent, and merits, of global capitalism.

Are nation states still important actors?

The four main views are differentiated by their assessments of the relative power of states and markets in global capitalism. The first view I will call the "globalization weakens the nation state" view. The nation state as an actor plays only a supporting role and is in danger of being shunted off-stage altogether. The second I call the "globaloney" or "states are still powerful" view: the state is still a leading actor. The third is the "some states are still powerful" or the "new imperialism" view, in which some actors have usurped the roles of others. The final view is the "regionalism is more important" view. In order to understand the play, a closer look at the changes to the stage is needed.

I will review each of these interpretations of global capitalism. One of the constant features of capitalism, evident throughout the history surveyed in this book, is its capacity to generate opposition. This has, historically, come from organizations formed by workers. New groups have more recently been evident, as environmental, anti-poverty and indigenous groups testify, to name only some. Contemporary opposition to "global capitalism" takes a multitude of forms, many of which are premised on different assessments of the key characteristics of global capitalism. In analysing the four views of global capitalism presented here, I will explore the implications of these views for the basis of opposition to this capitalism.

I. The "globalization weakens the nation state" view

The most well-known of the four views, it finds expression in the popular media as well as from politicians and from various think-tanks from both ends of the political spectrum. According to this view, the beginning of the twenty-first century is marked by an inexorable process of globalization driven by technological change. The global economy is seen as being formed by the activities of global firms which are able to operate globally because the information and telecommunications revolution allows them to possess, process and transmit huge quantities of information at very low cost and at very high speed. As an example of this revolution, the UNDP (1999: 28) provides the following figures for the average cost of processing information: in 1960, it cost US$75 per million operations; in 1990 it cost less than one hundredth of a cent. This has led to a dramatic change in the way in which businesses operate. They have "gone global". The period before 1985, say, was one in which national economies were linked together; now there are genuinely global firms, production and markets. Automobiles assembled from parts made in tens of countries and sold by corporations with annual sales larger than the national incomes of many states provide one of the more obvious examples.[3]

As a general description of the contours of the "new" global economy, this sketch would be acceptable to many supporters and opponents of globalization. After this, however, a sharp divergence of views would emerge about the implications and desirability of this agreed new "global reality".

All hail a twenty-first century utopia?

For supporters of globalization, the new global economy offers the prospect of rising living standards for all, through increased trade and the international diffusion of technology, and of the consolidation of democratic institutions. The interpretation offered here is that an open global economy offers the poorer countries the opportunity to "catch up" with the richer countries. Access to the technology embodied in the goods purchased from advanced countries and the technology which open borders bring with the multinational corporation are the main channels through which the appealing possibilities of "catch-up" occur.

Since technology is identified as the key to the emergence of the new global economy, the spread of technology is seen as the key to successful participation in this economy. The "digital divide", which separates regions and countries between those in which the new technology is fully operational and those where it is not, needs to be bridged and closed. What national governments must do, therefore, is maximize the flow of technology into their countries. The policies required to do this are preferably a package of trade and investment liberalization measures, security of property rights including intellectual property rights, low taxes on profits in order to encourage firms to operate in one particular jurisdiction rather than another, and a ready, subsidized, and low-taxed supply of highly trained workers. Any country which can offer this package would do very well in the new global economy.

The implication of this is that firms, mobile capital, have new power as the much sought-after providers of success in the global economy. International agreements, such as free-trade agreements, world trade liberalization and multinational investment agreements, are seen as providing the international architecture necessary to encourage the greatest spread of the benefits of global firms. These types of agreements tie the hands of national governments in many ways, ways which are viewed as beneficial by the supporters of globalization because they prevent interventionist politicians from interfering with the surest path to economic advancement. With "capital friendly" national governments and "capital friendly" international agreements, globalization is seen as delivering greater economic efficiency and higher levels of material well-being to all who participate. Capital is stronger, the state is weaker, but all benefit.

Supporters of globalization claim not only that all can prosper by participation in the global economy but that poor countries will benefit more than others. As a result, global income inequality is expected to decline. The argument here is that countries at lower levels of *per capita* income have the opportunity to grow faster than richer countries because they have a greater distance to go – and hence can increase productivity faster – to reach the technological frontier. This is "can" – not "must" – because this outcome is conditional on countries adopting the "appropriate" set of "capital friendly" policies. If this condition is met, then the prospects for increasing world equality are argued to be high. Consider, for example, the views of prominent Chicago economist Robert Lucas. He argues (2000: 116) that "ideas can be imitated and resources can and do flow to places where they earn the highest returns. Until perhaps 200 years ago, these forces sufficed to maintain a rough equality of incomes across societies (not, of course, within societies) around the world. The industrial revolution overrode these forces for equality for an amazing two centuries: That is why we call it a 'revolution'. But they [the forces of equality] have reasserted themselves in the last half of the 20th century, and I think the restoration of inter-society income equality will be one of the major economic events of the century to come." By 2100, Lucas muses, we could all be "equally rich and growing".

By implementing the same "capital friendly" set of policies, individual states are likely to become more similar, i.e. to converge in their institutions, and national differences are likely to be lessened. Since the policy package has most resemblance to the Anglo-American model of economic management, all countries will converge to this model. Furthermore, the power of global markets ensures that those countries which do not adopt this set of policies and converge to this model are brought to account. This is particularly the case with financial markets which are seen as acting as a warning siren that governments are pursuing policies which are inimical to growth; private investors lose confidence and withdraw their funds, causing a financial crisis. But the crisis is the result of misguided government policy; the markets are merely the messengers. This was the view taken by some of the Asian financial crisis; the markets raised the alarm about "crony capitalism". Instead of states regulating markets, markets now discipline states.

The supporters of globalization further predict not only a new global economy but also a new world of democracy accompanying it. Taking the "capitalism leads to democracy" argument presented in Chapter 2, and applying it to the contemporary period, leads Huntley (1998) to discuss the prospects for a twenty-first century *Pax Democratica*, in which the combination of globalization and democracy can lead to a new utopia.

Or, beware the "privatization of everything"?

For its opponents, global capitalism presents us not with a new utopia but with a new catastrophe, economically, socially, politically, culturally and environmentally. The rise of corporate power, and the increasing inability of nation states to control their activities as corporations become "stateless", present opponents with a frightening scenario for the twenty-first century. The drive for profits by global corporations opens up more and more areas of life to corporate or market control. The "capitalist system" has a seemingly infinite ability to expand into all areas of life. In the last chapter the "re-commodification" of health and education were given as examples of how the market is being reintroduced into critical areas in many core capitalist countries.

Everything becomes subsumed to the logic of private production for profit, according to opponents. Even forms of rebellion against capitalism, such as punk clothing or grunge music, soon become harnessed to the needs of the capitalist fashion and music industries. In the language of international trade agreements, "culture" becomes "cultural industries" and therefore subject to the predations of Hollywood and the media empires. Even countries attempt to "brand" themselves, as Peter van Ham (2001) puts it. According to him, "Singapore and Ireland are no longer merely countries one finds in an atlas. They have become 'brand states', with geographical and political settings that seem trivial compared to their emotional resonance among an increasingly global audience of consumers. A brand is best described as a customer's idea about a product; the 'brand state' comprises the outside world's ideas about a particular country" (van Ham 2001: 2). In the harsh world of attracting foreign investment and maintaining political influence, therefore, it is necessary for states to develop a good "brand image". "Public spaces" from classrooms to toilets increasingly become "privatized spaces" and legitimate sites for advertising (see Klein 2000). The continual assault on public space – in other words, its privatization – together with the established marketing principle that "sex sells", means that until there is "a cleavage on every corner" promoting all manner of goods, the relentless commodification of space will continue.

It is not only the privatization of space that is characteristic of this new phase of global capitalism. The privatization of life – its ownership by private firms – is also occurring. Vandana Shiva (2000: 118) argues that "with globalization, life itself has emerged as the ultimate commodity. Planet Earth is being replaced by Life Inc. in the world of free trade and de-regulated commerce. Through patents and genetic engineering, new colonies are being carved out. The land, the forests, the rivers, the oceans and the atmosphere have all been colonized, eroded and polluted. Capital now has to look for new colonies to invade and exploit for its further accumulation. These new colonies are, in my view, the interior spaces of the bodies of women, plants and animals." As a result, global corporations – Life Sciences corporations – are patenting life itself and seeking to control everything from the genetically modified food we eat to the medicine we take to the way we look.

As technology and the modern corporation combine to dominate the world, and as the ability of states to regulate them and protect citizens declines, what outcomes can we expect? Lucas's vision of an equally "growing and rich" world is no more than a cruel dream to opponents of globalization. They argue that, for individuals everywhere, it means greater economic insecurity as firms are increasingly able to dictate the terms on which employment is offered. It means the rise of contract labour, part-time work and shift work for those in core capitalist countries. Workers lose more and more control over their lives as the demands of the corporations for whom they work become both more stringent and less resistible. It means a flaunting of basic labour rights in developing countries as a "race to the bottom" occurs as countries compete with each other to offer global corporations the most obedient and low-paid workforces. And it means increasing inequality within and between countries. Core capitalist countries experience rising income inequality and governments become concerned with how to counter "social exclusion", the alienation of a significant part of the population from the mainstream of political and economic life. Newly capitalist Russia now has one of the highest levels of income inequality of any country, with the richest one-fifth of the population earning eleven times more than the poorest one-fifth (see UNDP 1999: 36). Inequalities between countries have also increased. In 1960 the richest fifth of the world's population earned 30 times more than the world's poorest fifth; in 1997, they earned 74 times more (see UNDP 1999: 36). This income inequality is matched by new patterns of environmental inequality. Globalization has led, according to Shiva (2000), to an "environmental apartheid", with resources going from the developing countries to the rich core countries but with polluting industries making the trek in the opposite direction.

Opponents point to the economic insecurity arising from the "global turbulence" caused by global financial markets as another prominent feature of this new stage of capitalism. The financial crises surveyed in the last chapter have wreaked havoc in many countries, both core and developing, over the past decade, bringing down governments, businesses and individuals in their wake. Markets are not seen as enhancing democracy but as destroying the ability of national governments to make independent policy choices. Global financial markets have become a "wrecking ball" for many societies; and this is even according to one of the chief wreckers, international speculator George Soros (1998), who argues that capitalism itself will be jeopardized unless a solution is found to the current situation in which "global markets" hold the upper hand over weakened states.

The resistance, and alternative, to a global capitalism interpreted in this way has focused primarily on the need to control global corporations and to regulate global markets using global institutions. Thus, policies aimed at introducing codes of conduct for corporations, for international labour standards, for international environmental standards and for taxes on international financial speculators are all premised on the need to limit the power of corporations to play states off against each other and to reclaim at the international level the regulatory role which states used to have. Global capitalism, and its promoting institutions such as the World Bank, the IMF and the WTO, need to be opposed by a global civil society implementing new forms of global regulation through global institutions. A "progressive globalization" is needed, it is advocated, to replace the present runaway global capitalism.

II. The "globaloney" or "states are still powerful" view

Far too much credence has been given to "globalization" according to this second interpretation. As an empirical matter, it is argued that the vast majority of production and investment – around 90 per cent – remain national in character. Firms and consumers are much more likely to trade with and purchase from fellow nationals than with foreigners. Furthermore, the share of government spending in the national incomes of the core capitalist economies shows no sign of being reduced (despite the best efforts of neoliberal governments such as those of Thatcher and Reagan to achieve this outcome). Adherents to this view also point to the fact that international markets, including financial markets, are now only just reaching the levels of integration which they attained in the late nineteenth century. What globalization there is, therefore, is hardly new. In short, to use political economist Robert Wade's (1996: 60) words, "reports of the death of the national economy are greatly exaggerated".

According to this interpretation, therefore, national economies are still the basic economic units of the global economy, economic activity remains deeply embedded in national structures, and states remain powerful economic actors. Even the conservative-minded flagship weekly *The Economist* agrees with this and has described the idea of the "powerless state" as a "myth".[4]

If it is the case that "globalization" is in fact "globaloney", then why is there so much talk about it? One explanation is that it is simply an intellectual fad, a populist catchphrase that has caught the popular imagination but which is likely to become redundant when the next fad comes along. Other fads – the "leisure society", the "peace dividend", for example – can be given as other popular concepts which have failed to stand the test of time. But this is not the only explanation for the prevalence of "globalization-speak".

A more sophisticated explanation suggests that while the case for globalization may not be terribly compelling empirically, its real purpose is to serve as an ideological weapon of the corporations and the neoliberal agenda. That is, what is occurring is not so much globalization, a technologically driven process, but global*ism*, an ideology.[5] This ideology is based on the neoliberal view that markets and firms *should* play the dominant role in the organization of capitalist economies and that states *should* play limited roles. The purpose of this ideology has been to get citizens to accept that "there is no alternative" and to promote what popular commentator Linda McQuaig (1998) has called a "cult of impotence". Governments could be more powerful if they wished but the ideological onslaught of neoliberalism, surveyed in the last chapter, has found in globalization a powerful and convenient argument that corporations must be allowed to have more power and that states must adjust to the imperatives of the global economy. It is for this reason, as an ideological tool to make citizens accept a restructuring of their working lives and a restructuring of the public services which they have claimed in the post-1945 period, that globalization has found such resonance amongst global elites. It serves the interests of the corporations and of the rich for everyone to believe that there is nothing that can be done to restrain the ability of corporations to have greater freedom to operate around the globe.

And while state elites, especially of the neoliberal persuasion, and corporations have been successful in persuading the doubters of the "inevitability" of globalization, they have also been actively dismantling the power of the state by liberalizing markets in order to give credence to that very "inevitability"!

Opponents of globalization who follow this interpretation tend to focus on the continued possibilities for national governments to control the course of events and to improve the lot of their citizens. A high level of national autonomy is still possible in the twenty-first century if the state can be captured by those willing to dispel the myths of neoliberalism and globalism, to regain some of the powers of the state given away to capital, and to use them for renewed progressive national projects. A "progressive nationalism" is needed.

III. The "some states are still powerful" or "new imperialism" view

A third view of globalization is that while it has weakened some states, it has enhanced the power of others and deliberately so. It is argued that the most powerful core capitalist countries, particularly the US, have used globalization as way of expanding their global power and the profitability of their corporations. Globalization – or the global spread of capitalism – is a project being carried out by core capitalist states in support of the interests of the capitalist system as a whole and multinational corporations in particular.

As radical critic Humphrey McQueen (2001: 210) has argued, "one of the few certainties about globalisation is that it is most often Americanisation. Its logic does not require the United

States to be borderless, only everybody else." This is the key point in this interpretation of globalization. It is a process which weakens only some states – the weakest. They either have forced on them, or have their neoliberal leaders willingly embrace, the market liberalization measures and privatizations which give greater reign to foreign capital. Meanwhile, the core states' positions are enhanced by the opening of more and more areas of economic activity in other countries to their firms. Globalization is therefore characterized by advanced capitalist states, financial capital (such as banks and investment funds) and multinational corporations acting in concert to open up markets overseas. These characteristics recall late nineteenth-century capitalism, that is, a period of imperialism.

The concept of "imperialism" suffers from the "non-naming syndrome" even more than capitalism. Acceptable in academic treatise on the nineteenth century, its association with Lenin's analysis has made it a term only rarely used to describe the policies of the world's only superpower in twenty-first century global capitalism. For McQueen (2001: 197), therefore, the term "globalization" is seen as a "public-relations gloss". The purpose of this gloss is to present "monopolising capitals as the outcomes of ineluctable forces of nature, rather than of contestable social practices, [which] helps corporations to elude the hostility sparked by the word 'imperialism'" (ibid.).

To see through this gloss and understand its workings, "globalization" needs to be "unmasked", according to radical sociologists James Petras and Henry Veltmeyer (2001). For them, the argument that globalization is "inevitable", and the result of the types of technological developments discussed in the "globalization weakens the nation state" view, is fundamentally misleading.

While accepting that technological change has taken place, they reject the claims that it is of such a large nature that it has of necessity revolutionized production methods. Indeed, the empirical evidence which they present points to the absence of any great technological breakthrough in productivity over the past few decades.

Globalization, for Petras and Veltmeyer, is not a technological imperative but a project of the ruling class to advance its interests. "Euro-American imperialism" describes a process in which the power of the US state and of leading European states is used to support the interests of the 37,000 multinational corporations in opening up world markets through trade and investment liberalization and privatization programmes.

"Free trade" is again the banner under which imperial powers seek to open up the economies of others. And just as imperialism in the late nineteenth century encompassed not just the economic and political spheres but also domination by the imperial powers' cultures and values, so too does imperialism at the beginning of the twenty-first century. And, of course, the willingness of imperial powers to use military force to ensure this domination is also common to both periods. Thus, globalization appears not as an objective description of what must "inevitably" happen, but as the political project of imperialism.

The response to this, Petras and Veltmeyer argue, cannot be to "make globalization work for everyone" – or a "progressive globalization" – as some have argued, since globalization, interpreted as imperialism, is a specifically designed project to benefit the capitalist class at the expense of everyone else. In short, "globalization" is aimed at, and relies upon, subjecting the mass of the world to the demands of corporations from the core capitalist countries. As such, opposition to "globalization" must take the form of class resistance, both nationally and internationally, to the power of imperialist states and their corporations. What is required, therefore, according to their argument, is a strategy to move to a post-imperialist, socialist alternative for the twenty-first century.

While radical critics of capitalism propose a renewal of socialism to provide an alternative future, there are other forms that "anti-imperialism" has taken. In some countries, such as France and Japan, there have been mild forms of opposition to some of the "cultural imperialism" of the US, although this has typically not questioned the system of "capitalist imperialism" which might underlie it. More strident opposition has come from some Islamic countries and movements. "Anti-imperialism" is pursued by violent means by some, most spectacularly in the case of September 11. There has been a recent surge in books about the "clash of civilizations", the "clash of fundamentalisms", and "McWorld versus Jihad" which set out the conflicts between American (or Western) power and values and Islamic resistance to it.[6] However, much of this resistance is anti-American and even anti-modern rather than necessarily anti-capitalist.

IV. The "regionalism is more important" view

The world is changing. But what are emerging are regional economic and political activities and structures rather than global activities and structures. The final interpretation presented here argues that regionalism is a more accurate description of the changes under way than globalization.

The view that contemporary capitalism is best described as regional rather than global rests on the strong regional biases to trade and investment flows as well as on the regional supra-national political structures which have been put in place. In terms of the former, while world trade and investment have expanded rapidly over the past two decades, there remains a strong regional bias in these flows. Regional economic integration agreements, for example, have increased dramatically over the past couple of decades.

The major regional blocs are Europe, the Americas and East Asia. European trade and investment has greatly increased as a result of the creation of the European Union, while intra-Asian and intra-Americas trade are also the dominant features of flows in these regions. Approximately 60 per cent of all trade in Europe is with other European countries, while intra-East Asian trade and intra-Americas trade are both approximately 30 per cent of total trade. Furthermore, while the Americas form a dollar zone, the euro is now Europe's currency and, arguably, there could be a yen zone in East Asia. To this evidence of economic integration must be added the political dimensions most evident in Europe with the European Union and the European Parliament. There are no comparable bodies in other regions. The North American Free Trade Agreement of 1994 between the US, Canada and Mexico and the proposed Free Trade Agreement of the Americas do point to the existence of a regional project, but its supra-national political structure is currently very limited. In Asia, the 10 members of the Association of South East Asian Nations (ASEAN), which was formed in 1967, created a free-trade area in 1992 and has now negotiated an agreement with China. The ASEAN countries have also joined with China, Japan and South Korea in putting in place mechanisms to assist each other in the event of another financial crisis similar to that which shook the region in 1997.

Interpreting contemporary capitalism as regional in character has led to questions about the nature of this regionalism. One question has been to examine the relationship between regionalism and globalization. Are they competing or complementary processes? This has typically been analysed in economic terms with the question being whether regional blocs are "stumbling blocs" or "building blocs" for the global economy. The fear of those who interpret regional arrangements as "stumbling blocs" is that we will witness a return to the insularity of the 1930s where imperial trading blocs were formed in an attempt to avoid the transmission of volatility from other regions. This fear finds expression in the descriptions of the EU and the NAFTA as creating "Fortress Europe" and "Fortress North America". For others, however, the "new regionalism" of the 1990s is characterized by its "openness" and its potential to spur greater global integration. On this reading, regionalism is part of the process of creating the global economy.

A further issue has been whether we are seeing the emergence of regional varieties of capitalism which have, in some important ways, succeeded the national varieties which were surveyed in Chapter 5. The issue here is whether we can identify in the Americas a US-style neoliberal capitalism being formed in contrast to a more social democratic, corporatist European model and a more limited, more networked East Asian version.

As indicated in Chapter 6, another issue which arose from this interpretation and which was particularly popular in the early 1990s was the view that there was an emerging tri-polar world capitalist system in which the post-1945 power of the US was disappearing. The agenda this raised was of how to forge cooperation and contain rivalries in this new period between the emerging rival capitalist regions. Now, increasing attention is paid to the rise of China.

Resistance to regionalism has sometimes taken the form of viewing regionalism as based on the same neoliberal ideology as "globalization" and therefore to be opposed on the same grounds. This has particularly been the case in North America where regionalism has also been dubbed "continental globalization", i.e., the dominance of capital over labour at the regional level. In Europe, the debate has been more centrally concerned with the relative powers of national versus European institutions and the extent to which progressive policies, involving a sharing of power between capital, labour and state, can be incorporated into the European movement.

The regional interpretation also allows for the national state to be weakened not only by the supra-national regionalisms but also by sub-national regionalisms. As the nation state has been weakened so more localized movements, based on ethnicity for example, have arisen to challenge the state. Many of these movements are conservative in nature and while they embrace globalization as it weakens the nation state they are often socially conservative in their own locales.

As the curtain falls: what drama is unfolding on the capitalist world stage?

"Globalization" has been interpreted in different ways and "anti-globalization" has taken many forms. But underlying all of these differences is the central debate with which we started this book. For globalization is still capitalism, although there is legitimate room to debate exactly how global it really is.

And global capitalism is still subject to the two differing assessments of capitalism which were presented in Chapters 2 and 3. For some, global capitalism is a "natural" evolution and offers the prospect of global "freedom". With capital-friendly policies, our drama can have a happy ending with humankind marching off into the sunset of global capitalist democracy. For critics, however, global capitalism merely intensifies and spreads further the "injustice" and the "instability". Unless the dictates of capital are tamed (for the reformists) or abandoned and replaced (for the radicals), the drama can only end as a tragedy.

Thinking about capitalism historically shows how global capitalism has arisen and what features might be new about it. Thinking about capitalism analytically demonstrates that "globalization" is still capitalism. Thinking about capitalism normatively still leaves judgements to be made.

In judging global capitalism, I am reminded of Keynes's 1931 review of a book by Hayek. In his review, Keynes (1972: 252) wrote that Hayek's ideas provided "an extraordinary example of how, starting with a simple mistake, a remorseless logician can end up in Bedlam".

This strikes me as an apt description of the characterization of capitalism as "natural and free". Markets in health which dictate that individuals who can pay will live and those who cannot will die are not "natural". Markets in food which deliver gastronomic delights to the rich and undernourishment for the poor are not "natural". "Human nature" does not dictate that these outcomes must prevail and human societies do not have to be organized in this way or human institutions work in this way. Markets are indeed "blind", as Hayek argued, but not in the way he suggested; rather they are blind to poverty, to environmental destruction and to inequality. Individuals who must give control of their labour to others are not "free". Individuals in the richer countries whose well-being depends on not losing their jobs, or on a family member not losing theirs, are not "free". Individuals in poorer countries whose well-being depends upon the price of their labour, or upon the price of what they produce not collapsing, or upon not being evicted from their land, are not "free". We can – and should – all be freer, and more human, than this.

Starting from the simple mistake that private property, the pursuit of profits and markets are the route to human freedom, the proponents of capitalism logically and remorselessly deduce that the relentless pursuit of profits, the ever greater accumulation of private property and the ever-expanding scope of the market – phenomena which characterize the contemporary phase of global capitalism – must enhance our freedom. They are more likely to lead us to Bedlam.

Further reading

There are shelves full of books on globalization. One of the best general introductions is Jan Aarte Scholte's *Globalization: A Critical Introduction*, New York: St Martin's Press, 2005. Ken Ohmae's book *The Borderless World*, London: Collins, 1990 has already become a classic for its vision of the demise of the nation state. Thomas Friedman's *The World Is Flat: A Brief History of the Twenty-First Century*, New York: Farrar, Straus and Giroux, 2005 continues the tradition and adds the twist that countries are now on a level playing field when it comes to competing in the global economy because capital is able to operate anywhere. A version of the "new imperialism" position is given in Leo Panitch and

Sam Gindin, *Global Capitalism and American Empire*, London: Merlin Press, 2004. A sceptical view on globalization (and more supportive of the regional interpretation) is offered by Paul Hirst and Grahame Thompson, *Globalization In Question: The International Economy and the Possibilities of Governance*, Cambridge: Polity Press, 1996.

Notes

1 This chapter is a revised and condensed version of Bowles (2005).

2 See Schaeffer (2002) and Friedman (2000), Mittelman and Othman (2001), Legrain (2002) and Went (2002), respectively.

3 For example, on the basis of this type of comparison, General Motors is larger than Thailand and Norway; Ford is larger than Poland; Toyota, Wal-Mart and Exxon are all larger than Malaysia, Venezuela and the Philippines. See UNDP (1999: 32).

4 See *The Economist*, "The myth of the powerless state", 7 October 1995, p. 15.

5 Fligstein (2001: 221) defines an ideology as "a set of ideas that reflect a point of view".

6 See Huntingdon (2002), Tariq Ali (2003) and Barber (1996) respectively.

References

Amsden, Alice (1989), *Asia's Next Giant: South Korea and Late Industrialization*, New York: Oxford University Press.

Aune, James Arnt (2001), *Selling the Free Market: The Rhetoric of Economic Correctness*, New York and London: Guilford Press.

Barber, Benjamin R. (1996), *Jihad vs McWorld*, New York: Ballantine Books.

Beaud, Michel (2001), *A History of Capitalism 1500–2000*, 5th edn, New York: Monthly Review Press.

Bowles, Paul (2000), "Regionalism and development after(?) the global financial crises", *New Political Economy*, 5(3), pp. 433–455.

Bowles, Paul (2005), "Globalisation and Neoliberalism: A Taxonomy and Some Implications for Anti-globalisation", *Canadian Journal of Development Studies*, XXVI, 1, pp. 67–87.

Bowles, Samuel and **Gintis, Herbert** (1976), *Schooling in Capitalist America: Educational Reform and the Contradictions of Economic Life*, New York: Basic Books.

Bowles, Samuel and **Gintis, Herbert** (1988), "Schooling in capitalist America: reply to our critics", in Cole, Mike (ed.), *Bowles and Gintis Revisited: Correspondence and Contradiction in Educational Theory*, New York: Falmer Press, pp. 235–246.

Boyer, Robert and **Hollingsworth, J. Roger** (1997), "From national embeddedness to spatial and institutional nestedness", in Boyer, R. and

Hollingsworth, J.R. (eds), *Contemporary Capitalism: The Embeddedness of Institutions*, Cambridge: Cambridge University Press.

Broomhill, Ray and **Sharp, Rhonda** (2003), "A new gender (dis)order?: Neoliberal restructuring in Australia", in Laxer, Gordon and Soron, Dennis (eds), *Decommodifying Public Life: Resisting the Enclosure of the Commons*, London: Zed Books.

Carter, Neil (2001), *The Politics of the Environment: Ideas, Activism, and Policy*, Cambridge: Cambridge University Press.

Clavin, Patricia (2000), *The Great Depression in Europe, 1929–1939*, Basingstoke: Macmillan.

Coates, David (2000), *Models of Capitalism: Growth and Stagnation in the Modern Era*, Malden, MA: Polity Press.

de Soto, Hernando (2000), *The Mystery of Capital: Why Capitalism Triumphs in the West and Fails Everywhere Else*, London: Bantam.

Elson, Diane and **Pearson, Ruth** (1981), "Nimble fingers make cheap workers: an analysis of women's employment in Third World manufacturing exports", *Feminist Review*, 87–107.

Engels, Friedrich (1962), "The part played by labour in the transition from ape to man", in *Marx and Engels Selected Works*, Volume II, pp. 80–91, London: Lawrence and Wishart.

Esping-Andersen, Gosta (1990), *The Three Worlds of Welfare Capitalism*, Princeton, NJ: Princeton University Press.

Ferguson, Niall (2001), "Globalization in historical perspective: the political dimension", Contribution to Panel Discussion in Bordo, M., Taylor, A. and Williamson, J. (eds), *Globalization in Historical Perspective*, NBER, book in progress.

Fieldhouse, D.K. (1981), *Colonialism 1870–1945: An Introduction*, London: Weidenfeld and Nicolson.

Fligstein, N. (2001), *The Architecture of Markets*, Princeton, NJ: Princeton University Press.

Folbre, N. (2001), *The Invisible Heart: Economics and Family Values*, New York: The New Press.

Friedman, Milton (1953), "The case for flexible exchange rates", in Friedman, Milton, *Essays in Positive Economics*, Chicago: University of Chicago Press.

Friedman, Milton (1990), "Using the market for social development", in Dorn, J. and Wang Xi (eds), *Economic Reform in China: Problems and Prospects*, Chicago: University of Chicago Press.

Friedman, Milton and Friedman, Rose (1962), *Capitalism and Freedom*, Chicago: University of Chicago Press.

Friedman, Thomas (2000), *The Lexus and the Olive Tree: Understanding Globalization*, New York: Anchor Books.

Fukuyama, Francis (1992), *The End of History and the Last Man*, London: Hamish Hamilton.

Galbraith, John K. (1967), *The New Industrial State*, Boston, MA: Houghton Mifflin.

Garside, W.R. (1993), "Introduction", in Garside, W.R. (ed.), *Capitalism in Crisis: International Responses to the Great Depression*, London: Pinter Publishers.

Gordon, David (1996), *Fat and Mean: The Corporate Squeeze of Working Americans and the Myth of Managerial Downsizing*, New York: Free Press.

Gray, Nigel (1985), *The Worst of Times: An Oral History of the Great Depression in Britain*, Totowa, NJ: Barnes and Noble.

Greenspan, Alan (1998), "The ascendancy of market capitalism", Remarks before the Annual Convention of the American Society of Newspaper Editors, Washington, DC, 2 April 1998.

Haber, S. (ed.) (2002), *Crony Capitalism and Economic Growth in Latin America: Theory and Evidence*, Stanford, CA: Hoover Institution Press.

Hall, Stuart (1988), *The Hard Road to Renewal: Thatcherism and the Crisis of the Left*, London: Verso.

Haseler, Stephen (2000), *The Super-Rich: The Unjust New World of Global Capitalism*, London: Macmillan.

Hayek, Friedrich A. von (1944), *The Road to Serfdom*, Chicago: University of Chicago Press.

Hayek, Friedrich A. von (1960), *The Constitution of Liberty*, Chicago: University of Chicago Press.

Heilbroner, Robert L. (1985), *The Nature and Logic of Capitalism*, New York: Norton.

Heilbroner, Robert L. (2000), *The Worldly Philosophers: the Lives, Times, and Ideas of the Great Economic Thinkers*, New York: Simon and Schuster.

Hobsbawm, Eric (1994), *Age of Extremes: The Short Twentieth Century 1914–1991*, London: Michael Joseph.

Hochschild, Arlie Russell (2000), "Global care chains and emotional surplus value", in Hutton, W. and Giddens, A. (eds), *Global Capitalism*, New York: The New Press, pp. 130–146.

Hodges, Tony (2001), *Angola from Afro-Stalinism to Petro-Diamond Capitalism*, Bloomington, IN: Indiana University Press.

Huntingdon, Samuel P. (2002), *The Clash of Civilizations*, New York: Free Press.

Huntley, James (1998), *Pax Democratica: A Strategy for the 21st Century*, Basingstoke: Macmillan.

Hutton, Will (2002), *The World We're In*, London: Little, Brown.

Jameson, Frederic (1991), *Postmodernism, Or the Cultural Logic of Late Capitalism*, Durham, NC: Duke University Press.

Kang, David C. (2002), *Crony Capitalism: Corruption and Development in South Korea and the Philippines*, Cambridge: Cambridge University Press.

Kennedy, Paul (1983a), "Strategy *versus* finance in twentieth-century Britain", in Kennedy, Paul, *Strategy and Diplomacy 1870–1945: Eight Studies*, London: George Allen and Unwin, pp. 87–106.

Kennedy, Paul (1983b), "Why did the British Empire last so long?", in Kennedy, Paul, *Strategy and Diplomacy 1870–1945: Eight Studies*, London: George Allen and Unwin, pp. 197–220.

Keynes, John Maynard (1972), "The pure theory of money: a reply to Dr. Hayek", in *The Collected Writings of John Maynard Keynes*, Volume XIII, London: Macmillan.

Keynes, John Maynard (1973), *The General Theory of Employment, Interest and Money*, London: Macmillan.

Klebnikov, Paul (2001), *Godfather of the Kremlin: The Decline of Russia in the Age of Gangster Capitalism*, New York: Harvest Books.

Klein, Naomi (2000), *No Logo: Taking Aim at the Brand Bullies*, Toronto: Knopf Canada.

Korten, David (1995), *When Corporations Rule the World*, London: Earthscan.

Legrain, Philippe (2002), *Open World: The Truth About Globalization*, London: Abacus.

Lehmbruch, Gerhard (2001), "The institutional embedding of market economies: the German 'model' and its impact on Japan", in Streeck, Wolfgang and Yamamura, K. (eds), *The Origins of Nonliberal Capitalism: Germany and Japan in Comparison*, Ithaca, NY: Cornell University Press.

Lenin, Vladimir (1948), *Imperialism, the Highest Stage of Capitalism: A Popular Outline*, London: Lawrence and Wishart.

List, Friedrich (1966), *The National System of Political Economy*, New York: Augustus Kelley.

Locke, John (1960), *Two Treatises of Government*, ed. P. Laslett, Cambridge: Cambridge University Press.

Lucas, Robert E. (2000), "Some macroeconomics for the 21st century", *Journal of Economic Perspectives*, Winter, 14(1), pp. 159–168.

Manow, Philip (2001), "Welfare state building and coordinated capitalism in Japan and Germany", in Streeck, Wolfgang and Yamamura, K. (eds), *The Origins of Nonliberal Capitalism: Germany and Japan in Comparison*, Ithaca, NY: Cornell University Press.

Marx, Karl (1954), *Capital*, Volume 1, London: Lawrence and Wishart.

McMillan, John (2002), *Reinventing the Bazaar: A Natural History of Markets*, New York: Norton.

McQuaig, Linda (1998), *The Cult of Impotence: Selling the Myth of Powerlessness in the Global Economy*, Toronto: Viking.

McQueen, Humphrey (2001), *The Essence of Capitalism: The Origins of Our Future*, Sydney: Hodder Headline.

Mittelman, James and **Othman, N.** (eds) (2001), *Capturing Globalization*, London: Routledge.

Moore, Michael (2002), *Stupid White Men*, London: Penguin.

Parker, Randall E. (2002), *Reflections on the Great Depression*, Cheltenham: Edward Elgar.

Petras, James (2002), "The imperial counteroffensive: contradictions, challenges and opportunities", *Canadian Journal of Development Studies*, 23(3), pp. 455–474.

Petras, James and **Veltmeyer, Henry** (2001), *Globalization Unmasked: Imperialism in the 21st Century*, London: Zed Books.

Polanyi, Karl (1944), *The Great Transformation*, Boston, MA: Beacon Press.

Rainforest Action Network (2003), "Rates of rainforest loss", available at http://www.ran.org/info_center/factsheets/04b.html.

Robbins, Richard (2002), *Global Problems and the Culture of Capitalism*, 2nd edn, Boston, MA: Allyn and Bacon.

Rostow, Walter W. (1960), *The Stages of Economic Growth: A Non-Communist Manifesto*, Cambridge: Cambridge University Press.

Rothermund, Dieter (1992), *India in the Great Depression, 1929–1939*, New Delhi: Manohar Publications.

Schaeffer, Robert (2002), *Understanding Globalization: The Social Consequences of Political, Economic and Environmental Change*, Lanham, MD: University Press of America.

Schiller, Dan (1999), *Digital Capitalism: Networking the Global Market System*, Cambridge, MA: MIT Press.

Sharp, Rhonda and **Broomhill, Ray** (1988), *Short Changed: Women and Economic Policies*, Sydney: Allen and Unwin.

Sheahan, John (2002), "Alternative models of capitalism in Latin America", in Huber, Evelyn (ed.), *Models of Capitalism: Lessons for Latin America*, University Park, PA: Pennsylvania State Press.

Shiva, Vandana (2000), "The world on the edge", in Hutton, W. and Giddens, A. (eds), *Global Capitalism*, New York: The New Press, pp. 112–129.

Silverman, Bertram and **Yanowitch, Murray** (2000), *New Rich, New Poor, New Russia: Winners and Losers on the Russian Road to Capitalism*, 2nd edn, Armonk, NY: M.E. Sharpe.

Smith, Adam (1976), *An Inquiry into the Nature and Causes of the Wealth of Nations*, Oxford: Clarendon Press.

Soros, George (1998), *The Crisis of Global Capitalism: Open Society Endangered*, London: Little, Brown.

Standing, Guy (1989), "Global feminisation through flexible labour", *World Development*, 17, 7.

Stilwell, Frank (2000), *Changing Track: A New Political Economic Direction for Australia*, Annadale, NSW: Pluto Press.

Strange, Susan (1986), *Casino Capitalism*, Oxford: Blackwell.

Streeck, Wolfgang (2001), "Introduction: Explorations into the origins of nonliberal capitalism in Germany and Japan", in Streeck, Wolfgang and Yamamura, K. (eds), *The Origins of Nonliberal Capitalism: Germany and Japan in Comparison*, Ithaca, NY: Cornell University Press.

Tariq Ali (2003), *The Clash of Fundamentalisms: Crusades, Jihads and Modernity*, London: Verso.

Terkel, Studs (1970), *Hard Times: An Oral History of the Great Depression*, London: Allen Lane, The Penguin Press.

Thurow, Lester (1996), *The Future of Capitalism*, St Leonards, NSW: Allen and Unwin.

UNICEF (2002), "A world fit for children", available at www.unicef.org.

United Nations Development Programme (UNDP) (1999), *Human Development Report 1999: Globalization with a Human Face*, New York: Oxford University Press.

van Ham, Peter (2001), "The rise of the brand state", *Foreign Affairs*, Sept/Oct, 80(5), pp. 2–7.

Wade, Robert (1996), "Globalization and its limits: Reports of the death of the national economy are greatly exaggerated", in Berger, Suzanne and Dore, Ronald (eds), *National Diversity and Global Capitalism*, Ithaca, NY: Cornell University Press.

Wallerstein, Immanuel (1979), "The rise and future demise of the world capitalist system: Concepts of comparative analysis", in Wallerstein, I. (ed.), *The Capitalist World Economy*, Cambridge: Cambridge University Press.

Weber, Max (1976), *The Protestant Ethic and the Spirit of Capitalism*, 2nd edn, London: Allen and Unwin.

Went, Robert (2002), *The Enigma of Globalisation: a Journey to a New Stage of Capitalism*, London: Routledge.

Index